BUILDING A

Glorious HOME

A Pathway to a Successful Marriage

FATAI KASALI

BUILDING **GLORIOUS** HOME

Copyright © 2014 Fatai Kasali

The author has asserted his right to be identified as the author of this work in accordance with the Copyright, Designs and Patents Act 1988.

All rights reserved. No part of this publication may be reproduced, stored in a retrieval system, or transmitted, in any form or by any means, electronic, mechanical, photocopying, recording or otherwise without the prior permission of the author.

All Scripture quotations, unless otherwise indicated, are taken from the Holy Bible, King James Version, Cambridge University Press, Oxford University Press, HarperCollins and the Queen's Printers.

Scripture quotations marked 'Phillips' are taken from The New Testament in Modern English, copyright © 1958, 1959, 1960 J.B. Phillips and 1947, 1952, 1955, 1957 The Macmillian Company, New York. Used by permission. All rights reserved.

Published in the United Kingdom by Glory Publishing

ISBN: 978-09926138-2-2

Acknowledgements

To God be the glory for the grace to complete this book. My grateful thanks go to the members of the Redeemed Christian Church of God, Glory of God Parish, Bristol, England, towards the writing of this book. I am indeed very grateful for all their supports.

I would like to acknowledge the immense encouragement from my wife, Felicia Ebunlomo. She was always positive and supportive during the period of writing this book. I thank God for my sons, David and Daniel, for their understanding and supports.

Introduction

Marriage was established by God almighty. The idea of marriage originated from God. Therefore, the secret of success in marriage is in the hand of God, the originator. Any principles, ideas, invention or philosophy applied to marriage, without God, as the central figure, is an effort in futility.

This book explores the pathway to successful marriage. It exposes the necessary spiritual skills for successful marriage. You will learn in this book that it is possible to have a marriage that is godly and filled with joy. You will also discover, in this book that understanding is the key to maturity.

Genesis 2:24
Therefore shall a man leave his father and his mother, and shall cleave unto his wife: and they shall be one flesh.

The above Bible verse indicates that marriage is between a man and a woman. Marriage is not between a boy and a girl. This implies that maturity is needed for a successful marriage. This is because marriage involves heavy responsibilities which can only be performed by matured adults.

Furthermore, this book emphasises the importance of prayer as one of the major keys for successful marriage. Through prayer, you will be able to touch those areas of your marriage that no human hand can reach. Marriage is a spiritual institution and it will require spiritual exercise to make it works.

It must also be made clear that marriage involves a lot of hard-work in order to build it up to the level that will glorify the name of God. In this book, you will discover some of the major hard-works required for successful marriage.

May God make your marriage a glorious one in Jesus name.

Contents

1 Foundations for Successful Marriage 9

2 The Reasons for the Duties 33

3 Understanding Your Spouse's
Need for Development 47

4 Plans to Consider 59

5 The First Love 75

6 The Straws of Marriage 89

7 Communication in Marriage 107

8 Power of Prayer 161

Chapter One

FOUNDATIONS FOR SUCCESSFUL MARRIAGE

The foundation for a family is laid when a man and a woman marry with a pledge to live together for the rest of their lives. God is the author of marriage and in the beginning He laid the foundations for marriage success.

According to the Bible, the following foundations were provided by God for any marriage to succeed.

1. FOUNDATION FOR SECURITY

"And the LORD God planted a garden eastward in Eden; and there he put the man whom he had formed."
Genesis 2:8

God put the first man and woman in the Garden of Eden, a secure place for them to live. In this garden, there was peace and nothing to make them afraid. The meaning of Eden is paradise, that is, a place of peace chosen by God.

The reason why God put them in the garden was to enable them to constantly live in His presence, so as to watch over them. This is the foundation for security for any marriage to stand. Unless a couple dwell in a God-chosen place, they will never have absolute peace. If you can establish your home in the place that God has chosen for you, you will always find peace there. God will always relate with you where He has located you. For your home to experience His peace, you must choose the geographical location following God's directives.

Adam and Eve did not choose for themselves where to live, because God chose for them. It is only God who knows the best area to live in to suit your marriage. A place that is suitable for one couple may not be good for another. If you get your location wrong, many things in your marriage will go wrong. Living in a wrong place will constantly expose your home to certain dangers.

For example, due to your circumstances, you and your spouse may need to live far away from where certain kinds of relatives and friends will not have easy access into your relationship. Some relatives and friends can threaten the existence of a home, especially when the marriage is young and the couple are still trying to understand what it means to be married. The two of them are vulnerable at this initial stage and the infiltration of wrong people into their marriage affairs may fuel problems, and the home comes under attack.

When you get married, ask God where your own Eden is. Every marriage has got its own Eden, where security is provided from every manner of attack.

2. FOUNDATION FOR SELF-SUFFICIENCY

"And out of the ground made the LORD God to grow every tree that is pleasant to the sight, and good for food;

the tree of life also in the midst of the garden, and the tree of knowledge of good and evil." **Genesis 2:9**

God made provision for what the first couple would eat. There was no lack of food. God wants His people to have abundant food to eat. God has made plentiful provision for your marriage survival where He has chosen for you to live with your spouse. If you miss your divine location, you will always struggle to have your needs met.

"When thou hast eaten and art full, then thou shalt bless the LORD thy God for the good land which he hath given thee." **Deuteronomy 8:10**

This verse shows that God wants His people to have more than enough to eat. It implies that it is not of God that a married couple will not have enough to eat. If God established your home, you will always have food to eat. *Philippians 4:19* says: *"… my God shall supply all your need according to his riches in glory by Christ Jesus."* If you continually lack food to eat as a family, you need to check what has gone wrong. It could be that God did not actually tell you to marry at the time you did, or you have moved out of your Eden – the place where He planted you and your spouse.

"Arise, get thee to Zarephath, which belongeth to Zidon, and dwell there: behold, I have commanded a widow woman there to sustain thee." **1 Kings 17:9**

God told Elijah to go and live in a specific place where all his needs would be met – God would bring provision to him. God is still using the same principle today with all His people, including married couples. You have to live where God has chosen for you, if He is to meet your needs. If your family is constantly finding it difficult to survive, you may need to ask God if you are living in a place He did not choose for you.

3. FOUNDATION FOR DIVINE HEALTH

"And the LORD God commanded the man, saying, Of every tree of the garden thou mayest freely eat: But of the tree of the knowledge of good and evil, thou shalt not eat of it: for in the day that thou eatest thereof thou shalt surely die." **Genesis 2:16-17**

Here in Genesis we see that God revealed to the first couple the root cause of sickness and death – disobedience. Unfortunately, since the Fall of Adam and Eve we all live in a fallen world where illness and death are a natural consequence of that first entry of sin into the world. However, through faith in Christ we can avoid disobedience of God and benefit from good health, healing and abundant life.

Sickness is an attack on marriage and it makes life difficult for the two spouses. Obedience to God will help you avoid many sicknesses. For example, the sin of gluttony can lead to obesity; the sin of drunkenness can cause cirrhosis of the liver; the sin of adultery can result in sexual diseases – not to mention the destruction of your marriage. There are also sicknesses that come from the enemy, especially if you have been involved in the occult in the past. Other illnesses are simply a natural feature of our fallen world, but we can still ask God for his healing.

If you or your spouse experience sickness that refuses to go, you may need to check if one of you has not eaten a 'forbidden fruit', whatever that might be in your life. God is the great Physician who can heal all our diseases, whether through medicine from your doctor or a miracle. Sometimes God asks us to endure illnesses for a time and a season, as suffering increases our dependency on him, and can refine our trust and faith in him (see *Romans 5:3-4*).

But if you avoid sin, you are less likely to become sick. Obedience is a foundation for sound health. Sickness was not in God's plan for the world he originally created, and it is not in his plan for the marriage He established – so we need to seek God for our healing, in prayer and in faith.

4. FOUNDATION FOR FRUITFULNESS

"And God blessed them, and God said unto them, Be fruitful, and multiply, and replenish the earth, and subdue it: and have dominion over the fish of the sea, and over the fowl of the air, and over every living thing that moveth upon the earth." **Genesis 1:28**

This verse shows that God blessed the first family and then told them to be fruitful. This implies that God empowered them to be fruitful through the blessings He invoked upon them. Every family established by God has been empowered by God to be fruitful. You received the empowerment the day you and your spouse stood in God's presence to be united in holy matrimony. God wants every family to be fruitful in all that they do for Him.

As far as physical fertility is concerned, it is only through being fruitful that the earth can endure. Without such fruitfulness, mankind would cease to exist. If you experience childlessness in your marriage, take it to God in prayer and seek the advice of your doctor. Even if you find that it is impossible to have children, with God nothing is impossible! Don't give up believing unless you feel God say that He has a different plan for your lives. But even if God doesn't choose to give you children of your own, He may ask you to adopt children, or foster them, or to be a father figure and mother figure to young people who lack role models or good parenting. Fruitfulness is not just about fertility – it is about being used by God to bless others.

Don't feel condemned if you are unable to have your own children. Some counsellors teach that you must have some unconfessed sin in your life, or more unhelpfully they say that God must be punishing you for the sins of your youth. But once you have confessed all, and repented, and you still don't get pregnant, what then? If God was punishing us for our sins, would anyone have children? We have all sinned and fallen short of God's glory, so the human race would come to an end!

The Bible reports that God opened Rachel's womb, and Sarah's womb and the wombs of the wives of several patriarchs. But the Bible does not teach that God will open the womb of every infertile woman or solve every man's infertility – that would be a perfection like Adam and Eve had in Eden, and perfection won't happen again until God creates a new heaven and a new earth at the end of time. In the meantime, we live in a fallen world, and although we have a miracle-working God, He is sovereign in how He chooses to work in our lives.

That said, God is always seeking to bless us. If there is no fruitfulness in any area of your family, you need to consult God as to what His plan is for your life. You and your spouse can live a fruitful life. Every home established by God receives His blessings to empower them for fruitfulness, in one way or another.

If you have married according to God's laid foundation, you and your spouse must have received blessings from the priest or pastor that coordinated your marriage ceremony. That prayer is a blessing that will empower your home to function gloriously. The blessings you receive on the day of marriage will continue to multiply as you continue to allow God to dwell in your home. If you have not married according to God's laid foundation, you need to revisit that foundation and do things right. Consult your pastor for help to find out what is wrong, in order to make things right.

5. FOUNDATION FOR ENDURING UNITY

"Therefore shall a man leave his father and his mother, and shall cleave unto his wife: and they shall be one flesh." **Genesis 2:24**

An enduring unity is only possible when it takes place between two people in a covenant relationship. The two partners are to come together to form a new entity, 'glued together' by their covenant commitment.

It is in the plan of God that two people who marry each other should live separately from their relatives. There should be no third party. The presence of a third party in your marriage will weaken the bond of unity in your home. The third party could be your friend or parent. The problem is that, after some time, the third party tends to be sentimental and takes sides. This begins in a subtle manner, gradually worsening until one of you in the marriage gets drawn to the side of the third party and enjoys his or her sympathy. This weakens the bond of unity between the two of you. If you think you need somebody to counsel you and your spouse, look for a neutral person who is filled with the Holy Spirit and has experience in marriage matters. You will lay a foundation for enduring unity if you and your spouse become one without any third party.

6. FOUNDATION FOR ENDURING LOVE

> *"And they were both naked, the man and his wife, and were not ashamed."* **Genesis 2:25**

God created Adam and Eve to live together unclothed. This complete physical nakedness implies a total spiritual openness and vulnerability to each other, involving perfect honesty, trust and giving, with genuine commitment.

For a couple to maintain their first love in marriage, they must maintain being naked towards each other, i.e. open about everything. If couples share a genuine commitment to complete honesty, trust and generosity with each other, love will flow naturally in such an atmosphere.

Concerns will arise when one individual begins to operate as a separate entity. Love is about giving of the heart to a person you love. For your heart to remain with the person you love there must not be anything that breaks the heart. When a heart is broken, it is always difficult to mend. Dishonesty, double standards, mistrust and lack of commitment will eventually break the heart. A love that will endure in all situations must maintain oneness of the heart through nakedness. Nakedness will enable a couple to love each other in all situations, both good and bad.

Many couples have stayed together despite poverty, sickness and every manner of hardship. What keeps their love going is openness of the heart. No hidden agendas. No separate visions. It is difficult to follow a person if you don't know where he is going. Where there is openness, love endures all situations.

Togetherness creates a sense of security. While it is mandatory to love each other, it should also be known that love flows naturally without pains of the heart where there is genuine oneness in all things. It is true that your spouse must love you in all situations, but you have the responsibility of ensuring that you don't give room to the Devil.

7. FOUNDATION FOR ACCEPTANCE

"And the LORD God said, it is not good that the man should be alone; I will make him an help meet for him.

> *And out of the ground the LORD God formed every beast of the field, and every fowl of the air; and brought them unto Adam to see what he would call them: and whatsoever Adam called every living creature, that was the name thereof. And Adam gave names to all cattle, and to the fowl of the air, and to every beast of the field; but for Adam there was not found an help meet for him."*
> **Genesis 2:18-20**

God brought different animals to Adam to see and examine, and to find out if any of them would make a suitable companion for him. Adam did not accept any of the animals as his "help meet". This phrase, 'ezer kenegdo' in the original Hebrew, means "one who is the same as the other and who surrounds, protects, aids, helps, supports." Animals could be of some help, but they could never match up to this. But when God brought Eve to Adam, Adam knew he had found his 'ezer kenegdo' – someone he could accept as his ideal companion.

There must be acceptance before marriage. This is the reason why courtship is suggested. It is during courtship that the two partners will be able to gain a deep understanding of certain areas of each other's life, in order to make a decision about the possibility of marriage. Courtship gives you the opportunity to discern the character and motives of the heart of the person you want to marry. Marriage comes in only after you have accepted everything about the person you want to marry.

While it is impossible for you to know everything about your spouse, there are certain vital areas of his or her life that you should be able to discover, in order to make the decision after thorough prayer. Make certain that God is telling you to marry the person, and ensure that you find out all you need to know about your prospective partner, because after marriage, there should be no turning back. All the concerns you may have must be sorted out before proceeding into marriage. Even if you are sure that God is telling you to marry the person, you must still satisfy yourself about all the questions you have before marriage.

If concerns arise after marriage, you will need to take them before God in prayer, asking Him to give you wisdom to deal with the issues. But it is mandatory that you accept your spouse as he or she is, otherwise, it will be counted against you as sin. Rejection is a sin. Acceptance is reflected in ignoring offence, tolerance, maturity, understanding and forgiveness. The person you do not accept will always irritate you. You will always have something about him or her to complain about. You must accept your spouse. You must accept his or her height, body shape, character, strength, weakness, family background, mental capacity, etc. This is a decision you must make before marriage.

8. FOUNDATION FOR MATURITY

> *"And Adam said, This is now bone of my bones, and flesh of my flesh: she shall be called Woman, because she was taken out of Man. Therefore shall a man leave his father and his mother, and shall cleave unto his wife: and they shall be one flesh."* **Genesis 2:23-24**

The above shows that marriage should be between a man and a woman, not a boy and a girl. This implies that maturity of personality is necessary in marriage because of the heavy responsibilities involved, in addition to the obvious physical maturity.

Maturity is demonstrated when a person responds to the circumstances or environment in an appropriate manner. This is not determined by age but experience of life, plus a willingness to learn. What life has taught you will determine the level of your maturity. It will add to your knowledge and will directly determine how you respond to situations in life. Your character is shaped by your maturity. Your level of maturity reflects in your decision-making, your ability to withstand pressure, your tolerance level and your emotional balance, as well as your ability to overlook offence and make correct judgements. All these determine if you are suitable for marriage.

Are you aware of how a man and a woman function differently in the same situations? Has life taught you about emotional differences between a man and a woman? Can you function well under stressful situations?

Due to all these circumstances, the Bible indicates that marriage should only be between a man and a woman. You may be elderly but still immature, while a man far younger than you can be more mature than you. The good news is that an immature person who has entered into marriage can learn about maturity. If you can bring yourself under the guidance of the Holy Spirit, He will teach you all that you lack in terms of maturity. You also must accept that you need certain teachings, otherwise you will be unteachable.

9. FOUNDATION FOR KNOWLEDGE

You need a certain kind of knowledge for your home to stand and be peaceful. If you can live by this basic knowledge as revealed by God in the beginning, you will be able to build a glorious home.

Which knowledge?

Genesis 2:23 says: "And Adam said, This is now bone of my bones, and flesh of my flesh: she shall be called Woman, because she was taken out of Man."

Adam was a man while Eve was called a woman. Understanding the difference between a man and a woman will lay a foundation for the knowledge needed to maintain your home. When you gain this knowledge, you will no longer take everything personally when your spouse behaves in the way that is normal for his or her gender.

1 Peter 3:7 says: "Likewise, ye husbands, dwell with them according to knowledge, giving honour unto the wife, as unto the weaker vessel, and as being heirs together of the grace of life; that your prayers be not hindered."

The happiness of your marriage will depend on how much you understand your spouse and react in a way that is appropriate to that understanding.

Let's compare the two: a man and a woman.

The Man

He was the first to be created by God. He was given a garden to take care of. He was to provide for his family and protect them. Man is naturally more aggressive because he is a hunter, given the responsibility of hunting for food for his family. Man is built with muscles and aggression to help him capture food animals and serve his family well. He occupies the position of a problem solver and every member of the family looks toward him for a solution to their problems. A woman must understand that a man is naturally built to be more aggressive and able to defend his family. Even a regenerated man still exhibits certain aggressiveness in many situations. There are chemicals and hormones inside a man that make him behave in a certain way that is different to a woman. A woman must dwell with a man with this understanding. When your husband exhibits certain attributes as a man, don't personalise it. If you feel uncomfortable with such attributes, you may advise him and also take it to God in prayer. You must also know that it is in the nature of man to feel superior to a woman because in the beginning man was created first. Male domination is therefore a feature of many societies where inequality between a man and a woman is accepted, whereas the Bible teaches that men and women are equal in God's eyes (see Galatians 3:28), though different. This egotistical attitude departs from a man after he has been broken down by the Holy Spirit, but it takes time.

The Woman

She was made from man. She was designed by God to bear and take care of children. A woman has the ability to make things grow – both good and bad, depending on the level of maturity. If you give a woman a little bit of sadness, she will multiply it and return it to you in a bigger size. A woman has the ability to nurture and keep things alive for many years. She can keep in her mind an event that took place many years ago. She is emotional because emotion is involved in love and a woman was made to maintain love because of her role as a child bearer.

She is called a weaker vessel in *1 Peter 3:17*. She is a weaker vessel by virtue of her emotional instability, not just her physical strength. There are certain hormones and chemicals inside a woman that influence her emotionally. Some of these chemicals are produced in the body of a woman periodically, while some are continually being secreted. A man must know that there are clear differences between the way a woman and a man will react under the same circumstances, irrespective of the level of spirituality. This is because the chemical compositions are not the same. When your wife comes under the influence of emotion, you should not personalise it. It is not about you but what makes her a woman.

These differences are what a man and a woman need to know before getting into marriage. Different reactions in the same situation can generate friction in marriage if there is a lack of understanding. Understanding will enable an individual to behave in an appropriate way under different circumstances. If you can build upon this knowledge, you will learn how to laugh over many matters that would otherwise generate division and arguments at home.

The diversity between a man and a woman makes marriage very interesting. This diversity can be turned into a treasure. You will discover that this diversity makes your spouse stronger where you are weaker and vice-versa. This is called complementarity, and serves to strengthen your marriage, if you allow it.

There are things you need for life that God has not given you but He has put it in the life of your spouse. When you come together in marriage, you begin to exchange treasures for treasures. What your spouse needs, God has put in you, and you will release it to him or her and vice-versa. This will be a continual experience as both of you pass through life. It means that you will always need each other and neither of you will be a complete person without the other.

Commonality

Both man and woman are human beings created by God. Therefore there are certain features they have in common that must be respected by each individual in the marriage relationship. No matter how spiritual your spouse may be, you must know that he or she is a human being.

For example, it is the nature of a human being to feel pain, and when the pain is continuous the person will lose his composure and become irrational. Human beings can't function properly under pain, no matter the level of maturity. Therefore, you should not subject your spouse to painful experiences, otherwise you will drive your partner away from you. If your spouse becomes irrational, you need to check whether he or she is passing through pain.

Similarly, every human being possesses self-esteem that must be respected, so your spouse will need to be treated with a certain level of respect. Therefore, you should know that your spouse will be demoralised if you continually disrespect him or her and treat him or her like a dog. Also, because your spouse is only human, he or she has got feelings. Humans react to external stimuli with different emotions. The environment you create in your marital home will affect how your spouse functions, both emotionally and mentally.

Therefore, for you to get the best out of your spouse, you must establish a friendly atmosphere at home. It is important that you don't give the Devil a chance in your marriage and you should not become a source of temptation to your spouse. Your spouse has not got unlimited ability to cope with adversity. He or she has a breaking point. At a certain stage, he or she will not be able to take it anymore. In *1 Kings 19:1-4*, Elijah reached his breaking point – where he could not take any more battles. Don't push your spouse too far and don't exploit the fact that he or she is a good Christian. No one enjoys stress. You must avoid stressing your spouse because, under continuous stress, even the best person will lose his or her temper or begin to break down.

Spiritual foundation

The kind of people that an individual interacted with during childhood has a lifelong impact. Adam and Eve never grew up because they were created as adults. The only other person they knew was our perfect and holy God, so they had no experience of evil. This made it easy for the Devil to manipulate them.

The kind of a spirit a person interacted with as a child will give shape to his or her personality. You must find out how your spouse was brought up in life, before you met. This knowledge will enable you to understand how certain weaknesses and strengths entered into his or her life. For example, a child brought up by a single parent will lack certain skills needed in relationships, unless there was a strong presence of other adults, like grandparents. If you were not brought up by two parents, it may have created certain holes in your emotional and relational development.

We grow up to practise what we saw our parent or parents practising. A child of a single parent has interacted with the spirit that rules the life of a single parent. When he or she gets married, the spouse may discover that he or she does not know how to relate with some people, especially family members. It is not his or her fault. It is because he or she has not seen how a man and a woman live together in the same house and how they treat each other.

There may be lack of appreciation. All your effort to please him or her may fail. There may be a lack of respect. After all, this person has not been shown how to treat a wife or husband. The person may like individualism, always preferring to do things alone, especially if he or she was brought up as an only child. No one ever showed him or her how to live in unity with other people. Such a person may threaten the partner with divorce, even over a minor problem. This kind of problem arises because of the foundation set in childhood. If the person's parent was single because of divorce (as opposed to death of the spouse), the spirit of divorce has been transferred into his or her life through the way he or she was brought up.

Also, a person raised by a single parent or a divorcee may develop a wrong mind-set towards the opposite sex. If your spouse is a woman and was raised by a mother who had suffered at the hand of her husband before she was divorced, she may have developed a wrong mind-set towards men (equally, a boy raised by a single father may not know how to relate to women properly). She may distrust men due to what she saw her mother experience from her father. She will bring this wrong mind-set into your marriage. You may discover that she finds it hard to trust you and she suspects every move you make, even though you have the best of intentions.

These are the kind of problems you may need to fix as early in your marriage as possible, if you married a person brought up by a single parent or a divorcee. A child brought up by a divorcee will be sympathetic towards divorce when he or she gets married, even if she or he knows the Bible teaches it is wrong. It is a foundational problem. You must be aware that it was not anybody's fault. Few people choose to be a single parent, and it is not the child's fault if she or he is brought up by a single parent. Sometimes in life, bad things happen to good people. Some people are unfortunate to marry wrongly, although some become single parents because they lack what it takes to maintain marriage.

Furthermore, your spouse may even have been brought up in a polygamous home where the father had many wives.

This implies that your spouse had been interacting with the spirit that rules a polygamous home. Such a spirit breeds dissatisfaction, rivalry, suspicion, individualism and every manner of disorder. Such a person may find it hard to appreciate love. Unless the person has been truly delivered and fully regenerated, he or she may manifest the traits of the spirit that rules in the polygamous home in his or her own matrimonial home. The chance of divorce is high and there is the possibility of ungodly pressure from the person's parental home. When you notice any of these traits in your spouse, don't take it personally, but take it to God in prayer.

It is also important to mention that a child brought up in another religious environment such as Islam or idolatry has interacted with the spirit of religion for many years. While it may be true that the person is now a Christian, it would be no surprise if such a spirit manifests in his life. Unless there is a record of deliverance after accepting Jesus, there is a possibility that any of the ungodly spirits that the person has interacted with for many years in his parental home might not have been totally expelled from his life. If a certain spirit ruled in a home, then every child raised in it would need to undergo deliverance after accepting Jesus, so as to expel that spirit.

In some homes, there is a history of a particular sickness or bad event. In some homes, every person born there will experience hardship at a certain stage of their lives. In some families, it is common to die young, while in another home it is a common thing to be a late achiever. No matter how hard they try in life, they always achieve their success very late. The spirit that rules certain homes distributes certain afflictions to members at certain stages of their lives. When you notice that your spouse is manifesting any of the traits of these ungodly spirits, take it to God in prayer without taking it personally. Let your spouse go for deliverance and let the blood of Jesus be used to expel any of the spirits of his or her father's house that is still remaining in his or her life. Whatever spirit operates in the father's house, the power of the name of Jesus, with knowledge, will conquer them.

For example, in the father's house of Abraham, the spirit of barrenness was in operation. The Bible says Sarah was barren (*Genesis 11:30*); Rebekah, the daughter in-law of Sarah, was also barren for some years (*Genesis 25:21*), and Rachel, the daughter-in-law of Rebekah, was barren for a number of years (*Genesis 30:1*). This was a problem which originated from the father's house and needed to be fixed spiritually. Some homes have a history of anger; every child that grew up in such homes suffers from anger. This moral defect will follow the person to his or her marital home unless the spirit of anger is dealt with seriously.

For example, the homes of Simeon and Levi suffered from anger, as shown in *Genesis 49:5-7*, and this brought violence into their lives. Moses was from the family of Levi, as shown in *Exodus 2:1-10*, and the spirit of anger followed him into his ministry. He killed an Egyptian, was often angry with the people of Israel (e.g. *Exodus 16:20; Exodus 32:19; Leviticus 10:16; Numbers 16:15*) and he was prevented from entering the Promised Land (*Numbers 27:12-14*) because of disobedience, probably due to his temper.

Furthermore, some homes have a history of adultery, and every child that grew up in such a home will manifest this spirit as they journey through life. They are quick to seek divorce and remarry. The spirit of the father's house organises situations that will be used to lead them into adultery. It may be true that you and your spouse are born again, but you must know that giving your life to Jesus does not automatically expel all these wrong spirits from your life. They will still attempt to follow you through life; until you use the authority you have been given as a Christian to expel them.

Giving your life to Jesus gives you the believer's authority to put the devil where he belongs. You can still have authority and not use it, due to ignorance. If you assume that coming to Jesus has delivered you from all these wrong spirits, you are under self-deception. You have to let the devil know that you are a new creature and that you don't want to operate your life with the spirit of your father's house. You have to use the name of Jesus and the blood of Jesus shed on Calvary to put the devil where he belongs. Many Christians, who fail to do this, carry on living lives messed up by the Devil. Some Christians are barren today because they have failed to expel this spirit that follows them from their father's house. There are many Christian homes that are engulfed in divorce, hardship, sickness and a series of demonic manifestations. All these could be traced to their blood line.

It is also important to mention that some people were taken to witch doctors for spiritual assistance and protection by their parents when they were young. Unfortunately, such children had been dedicated to a certain spirit to serve as their spirit husband or wife. The witch doctors did not tell the parents that there is no free gift in the kingdom of the devil: there is always a price tag for every assistance received from the devil. Such children will grow up oblivious of the fact that they have been dedicated to certain spirits to be their wives or husbands. Later in life, they will get married and the spirit that they were dedicated to will start claiming ownership over their lives. This spirit starts generating a crisis that will make the marriage fail. Examples of such a crisis could be incessant misunderstandings between the couples, barrenness, serious financial hardship, sickness and miscarriage. In some cases, divorce becomes inevitable. This spirit is still claiming the legal right to enter into the life of this person because the name of Jesus and the blood of Jesus have not been used to expel it from the person's life.

If you notice all these strange events in your marriage, consult your pastor for deliverance and counselling.

Chapter Two

THE REASON FOR THE DUTIES

"Wives, submit yourselves unto your own husbands, as unto the Lord." **Ephesians 5:22**

"Husbands, love your wives, even as Christ also loved the church, and gave himself for it." **Ephesians 5:25**

In the beginning, God laid the foundation for marriage, as described in Genesis. He made it clear that men and women are different, so it is no surprise that they have different roles within marriage. For example, he obviously created women to bear children, not men. But in the New Testament, God gives us much more detail about the duties of each of the spouses in a marriage.

According to *Ephesians 5:22*, wives are to submit to their husbands, while in *Ephesians 5:25*, husbands are commanded to love their wives like Christ loves the church. These duties are mandatory and not subject to amendment, if a marriage is to succeed.

The first thing to say is that submission does not imply inequality. Men and women are equal in God's sight

(*Galatians 3:28*). So why should wives be commanded to submit, but husbands to love? What is in a man that will need continual submission from his wife in order for the marriage to stand? What is in a woman that will need continual love from her husband in order for the marriage to stand?

THE BRINGING OF THE WOMAN

"And the rib, which the LORD God had taken from man, made he a woman, and brought her unto the man."
Genesis 2:22

This verse states that, at creation, the Lord brought Eve to Adam to be his wife. This tradition still persists till today. Whenever marriages take place, the woman is always the one that will be brought to the man. In British wedding culture, it is the woman who is given away by the bride's father, and it is the woman who walks down the aisle to the man – who waits for her to arrive.

In *Genesis 24:58*, when the family of Rebekah agreed that she should marry Isaac, she went with the servant of Abraham to join Isaac. Traditionally, women have always been expected to join the families of their husbands. The consequence of this is that the woman goes to live in the midst of unfamiliar people until she understands them; and this usually takes time. She moves out of her father's house to the house of her spouse. She is also expected to change her surname to his. The man, in contrast, stays with his own people. He will maintain his surname and have free and continual access to the people that he has got used to over the years.

Although modern cultural changes have interfered with this tradition, it still holds true in most places. And it subtly affects the nature of the spouses as they live together as husband and wife. It shapes their mentality and expectations towards each other. We shall consider each of the spouses separately, to give better understanding.

THE WOMAN

"Husbands, love your wives, even as Christ also loved the church, and gave himself for it." **Ephesians 5:25**

The woman is now mixing with unfamiliar people – her in-laws. Therefore, she has concerns about security. Every woman desires security. This nature is inherited from generation to generation among women, and goes back to the time of the first woman that ever lived – Eve. As a husband, you must understand that your wife needs security. She has come to live with you and among people that she is not familiar with.

God expects men to show love to their wives (*Ephesians 5:25*) because it is only love that gives assurance of security. You must show love to your wife until she is fully convinced that you truly love her. We may take it as a given in our culture that men and women marry for love. But it certainly has not always been the case, and still isn't in many cultures, where wives are treated almost as commodities to be traded, or where marriages are arranged for reasons of social standing rather than love. So this command is very necessary. It removes the wife's fear of insecurity.

You must also understand that as your wife bears more children, she will need more security, as she worries not only about her own security but that of her children. She will exhibit this nature more and more, as she stays longer with you in the marriage. This is the reason why your wife will always ask you to verbalise that you love her. You may know it's true, but she needs to hear it! She will always desire this acknowledgement from you, irrespective of the number of years you are married. You will begin to notice a change only when her children are fully established in life, and she can relax a bit more.

When a woman is not receiving any security through her husband, she will be tempted to help herself to secure her future. Many women have been driven into adultery and excessively hard work in order to feel secure. Therefore, as her husband you must live a life that assures your spouse of security. You must aim to be an achiever. You must be a purpose-driven person, not lazy. You must take care of your wife and look after her as a jewel. You must ensure that your parents accept her as part of the larger family; otherwise she will feel more and more unsecured. Also, you must be progressive in life. You must be a provider for your home. If your wife discovers that you are too slack and don't care about providing a stable income and a secure home, she will begin to feel more insecure. No woman feels protected in a marriage with an uncaring man.

Here is a list of the things you should never do to your wife, otherwise you will increase her insecurity as she lives with you.

1. **Never threaten her** (verbally or physically, intentionally or unintentionally, knowingly or unknowingly). Threats will increase her sense of insecurity. It is in the nature of women to react to words; most women take every word seriously.

2. **Never flirt with other women.** She will always worry that she has a competitor for your affections. This causes more insecurity. And of course never commit adultery, which alone can break a marriage. But even if she forgives you and takes you back, she will be even more likely to worry about every friendship you have with other women.

3. **Never make her think that she is not first in your life.** Don't exalt your friends or relatives above her. Remember that she has left her family behind in order to marry you. She even changed her surname because of you (in most cases). She chose you above everything and everybody. She deserves to be first in your life.

4. **Never use her limitations and secrets to abuse or oppress her.** Otherwise, she will feel unable to trust you with any of her secrets, which will make her more insecure.

5. **Never withdraw from her when she faces difficulty.** Loneliness in the time of challenges will make her feel insecure and helpless in life.

6. **Never let her know if your relatives and friends don't like her.** Otherwise, she may start withdrawing from them due to insecurity.

7. **Never break her confidence in you.** Remember that when confidence is lost it will take a lot of time and effort to recover it.

8. **Never make references to her past offences.** Be quick to forgive her, otherwise you will make her feel more and more insecure in the marriage. If she discovers that you have not forgiven her for a past offence, she may start misinterpreting your behaviour, thinking you intend to pay her back in some way. That will make her more insecure.

9. **Never be secretive with her.** Be transparent. If she discovers your hidden secrets she will become insecure due to a lack of trust.

10. **Never publicly show anger to her.** Otherwise, she will not be comfortable with you in public due to fear of bad treatment. Women rarely forget public embarrassment from their spouses.

11. **Never be incessantly judgemental of her.** Otherwise, she will be lukewarm in relating with you due to fear of offending you. Learn how to correct in love.

12. **Never create a low self-esteem in her.** Give positive comments about her. Make her feel confident and secure with you.

13. **Never be un-pleasable to her.** Avoid being too demanding, otherwise she will think you don't love her genuinely. Let her little efforts satisfy you as much as major achievements.

14. **Never subject her to bullying – whether verbal or physical.** She will either break down emotionally and it may be difficult for her to recover, or she will react with fear or her own aggression. Domestic violence is of course abhorrent and completely unbiblical, in addition to being illegal.

15. **Never magnify her weaknesses above her strengths**, otherwise you may damage her self-image and she will feel belittled in the relationship.

16. **Never ignore any of her good efforts in the marriage.** Learn how to give good compliments. Acknowledge her good attempts at all things, whether she succeeds or fails.

17. **Never compete with her over anything.** Don't demand something because she also demands it. Competition will make her feel more insecure in your house.

18. **Never ignore her concerns.** Have listening ears. She will feel more insecure if she can't get you to acknowledge and address her concerns.

19. **Never use guilt as a weapon**, otherwise she will lose the liberty of relating with you because of the consciousness of sin. In addition, she may begin pointing out all your shortcomings too! Such tit-for-tat exchanges are never good for a marriage.

20. **Never be stingy to her.** Stinginess will make her feel that you don't love her enough, and that she has no one to take care of her if she needs greater help in the future. Be a provider.

21. **Never be unfriendly to her.** Women love men of humour.

22. **Never be negative, even in a negative situation.** Create hope and faith in the midst of uncertainty, otherwise you will open the door to doubt, and doubt breeds insecurity.

23. **Never take her insecurity personally.** It is not about you, but her natural self.

24. **Never call your wife bad names.** Avoid name-calling such as stupid woman, bad mother, greedy person, etc. Such name-calling will make her feel unloved, so she may look elsewhere for that love.

25. **Practice this always:** *"Charity suffereth long, and is kind; charity envieth not; charity vaunteth not itself, is not puffed up, doth not behave itself unseemly, seeketh not her own, is not easily provoked, thinketh no evil; rejoiceth not in iniquity, but rejoiceth in the truth; beareth all things, believeth all things, hopeth all things, endureth all things. Charity never faileth: but whether there be prophecies, they shall fail; whether there be tongues, they shall cease; whether there be knowledge, it shall vanish away"* (1 Corinthians 13:4-8).

THE MAN

"Wives, submit yourselves unto your own husbands, as unto the Lord." **Ephesians 5:22**

Wives are expected to submit to their husbands. The question is: what is it about a man that needs submission from a woman in order for the marriage to work?

In *Genesis 2*, man was the first to be created. Eve was brought to him as a wife. The same tradition still exists today in marriage. The man maintains his surname even after marriage (though a minority of women nowadays choose not to take their husband's name). In traditional cultures, he stays near to his own family even after marriage, though in modern, industrialised economies this has often broken down as the married couple have to move to wherever their work lies.

Nevertheless, the man seems to be in an advantageous position when it comes to marriage, in that it is the wife who takes his name, etc. This creates a feeling of superiority in man. Yet marriage is not designed to do that – it is designed to fulfil the needs of both the man and the woman, and give children the best upbringing they can have. Women have just as much to gain from marriage as a man, in fact, probably more. If husbands are supposed to love their wives as much as Christ loves the Church; that involves a huge self-sacrifice on behalf of the man that is not asked of the woman!

But since the Fall of humankind, men have always felt superior to women, especially when it comes to marriage. This is all about their ego. Ego is the false identity of self. It is a personal exaggeration of a person's identity. Men feel superior to women in marriage, yet they shouldn't. Submission is not about superiority. Despite Western laws on equality, most cultures in our world support the idea that men are superior to women, whether openly or in a more subtle way. This ego is the Adamic, fallen nature at work in man. Even born-again Christians suffer from ego issues when it comes to marriage. It takes the power of the Holy Spirit to remove it from genuine Christians. The reality is that it takes time for a genuinely born-again man to accept equality with his wife.

God expects a woman to be submissive to her husband because it requires humility to maintain a close relationship with a person who suffers from his ego. Only a humble person can tolerate a man who is filled with high self-esteem, or pride. That is why a woman can never succeed in changing her husband if she applies force or rudeness to the man. It is only the power of humility that can win over such a man. It requires humility to be submissive to a fellow human-being. Unless a woman is submissive to her husband, she will not have a good marriage. In our Western culture, it may be difficult to accept such submission – but it is to a woman's advantage to do so. It is no coincidence that the failure rate of Western marriages has increased since the concept of submission was undermined by strident feminism.

The power of humility is so strong that it can win over even a stubborn person. A genuinely humble person is always respected by people. As you become more and more submissive to your husband, you will soon notice that he will always make an effort not to offend you. He will have a higher regard for you. Humility begets honour, at least among Christians. Some non-Christian husbands might take advantage of submissiveness, but a Christian husband who is commanded to love his wife will instead feel honoured and privileged by his wife's submissiveness, especially in a nation where submission is frowned upon.

Due to his ego, there are certain things a woman should never do to her husband. These include the following:

1. **Never threaten your husband with divorce.** If you do that to a man who seriously suffers from egotism, he will feel little motivation to remain in the marriage. His ego will deceive him into considering such a word a challenge, and he may choose to seek a way of making you regret such a word. This could be the beginning of marital crisis.

2. **Never make your husband feel dependent on you.** Avoid treating him in a way that will make him feel that you think he can't do without you. His ego will deceive him into thinking that he is no longer free, and so he needs to free himself from the marital bondage he has entered into.

3. **Never make incessant corrections to your husband.** Avoid always faulting and blaming him. His ego will make him feel abused and that you consider him to be a fool. A man of ego always interprets correction wrongly.

4. **Never compete with your husband over anything.** If you do, he will turn the home into a race track where people compete for glory. Unhealthy competition makes a partner wish evil on their spouse, so that they lose.

5. **Never enforce your view.** Avoid always trying to win an argument. Don't always want to have the last word in any discussion with your husband. The ego in him may make him consider that you are disrespectful to him.

6. **Never disrespect the friends and relatives of your husband.** If you do, he may find it difficult to forgive you, unless he is genuinely born-again and has a strong relationship with the Lord.

7. **Never attempt to be in charge of every situation at home.** Always seek his permission, even if you think he won't mind what choice you make about something. An ego-driven man will feel oppressed if it seems as if his wife brushes him aside on issues that will affect him.

8. **Never make the weaknesses or limitations of your husband public.** The ego in him will make him feel that you are intentionally destroying his good reputation. If you think you need the intervention of an external person to help you in your marriage, invite only the person you know your husband respects.

9. **Never call your husband bad names.** Avoid name-calling such as stupid man, stingy person, lazy man, etc. Such names will hurt his ego and make it difficult for him to forget such bad names, so he may not be able to easily forgive you.

10. **Never compare your husband with another man outside your marriage.** If you did, he will feel greatly insulted. Men love being seen as incomparable in their marriage.

11. **Never use your advantage over your husband.** These may include sex, financial position, or certain opportunities. Don't withdraw family support because of some offence. His ego may make him feel small and

consider another relationship where sex is freely given, or he is the bigger earner or has more opportunities in life.

12. **Never blame your husband for your problems.** Avoid telling him that his incompetence brought you into your present problem. He may avoid supporting you in the future. Ego-driven men operate under the deception that they can never get things wrong.

13. **Never appear to be always right or as though you know everything.** Men love to be considered as solution providers. Some men feel small when their wives claim to have solutions to their marital challenges.

14. **Never demand appreciation from your husband for things you have helped him with.** He may reject future assistance from you in order to prove his supremacy. Let appreciation come naturally from him.

15. **Never declare a battle of supremacy against your husband.** Avoid telling him: "We shall see who will be the first to surrender or who will be the first to apologise." His ego will harden his heart and he will never surrender. This may be the beginning of a serious marital crisis.

An ego-driven person is not totally broken by the Holy Spirit and there are certain things he will not be able to tolerate. This is due to a lack of the maturity required to run a home effectively. It takes time for a man to be changed by the Holy Spirit. Therefore, as a wife you need to recognise this fact and incorporate it in your dealing with your husband. Through the power of the Holy Spirit, an ego-driven man can be transformed into a man of humility, but it usually takes time. Allow God to change your husband. Only God can change a man.

> *"Whoso findeth a wife findeth a good thing, and obtaineth favour of the LORD."* **Proverbs 18:22**

This verse declares that you are a "good thing" in your husband's home! It is one thing to be a good thing; it is another thing to remain a good thing. The devil always wants to contaminate a good thing. Your husband's ego could be used by the devil to turn you into a bad thing. You need to make a personal decision that you will not allow the devil to contaminate you through your husband's character defects. It requires humility to submit and cope with an ego-driven person. Your humility will train your husband in how to relate correctly to his "good thing". That is the beauty of submission.

Chapter Three

UNDERSTANDING YOUR SPOUSE'S NEED FOR DEVELOPMENT

> *"But if any provide not for his own, and specially for those of his own house, he hath denied the faith, and is worse than an infidel."* **1 Timothy 5:8**

Provision for the family is the joint responsibility of both partners. This is because every member of the family needs to develop and this will only be possible if certain needs are met.

A human being (whether male or female) is made up of body, soul and spirit. Therefore, for a balanced development, we must take care of all three of these areas. The body, soul and spirit must be developed in order to produce a complete, whole person. As our soul includes both our emotions and our mind, this implies that we need balanced development in four areas: the physical, emotional, mental and spiritual aspects of our lives. For a successful marriage, each spouse must develop in all these ways, otherwise there will be negative effects on the family.

A. PHYSICAL DEVELOPMENT

Obviously this concerns the physical body of an individual. You must provide whatever is needed for the physical well-being of your spouse. This begins with quality food to keep the body healthy. The family must eat a balanced diet. The kind of food you eat will affect how your body is maintained and functions. Your family must be well fed. *Exodus 16:12* shows that God provided bread and meat for the Israelites in the desert, and they ate until they were full. Children that lack certain vitamins will experience poor body development. A family that always eats only one type of food will not grow well physically. Don't starve your home because you have other things you are financing.

Secondly, you must allow your spouse to rest, and ensure your children get adequate sleep. The body needs rest, otherwise it will age more quickly and break down more easily. The body needs rest to refuel and for bones and muscles to relax. Encourage your spouse to get enough sleep, to allow his or her body to recuperate and recover. Don't allow your spouse to work more hours in a day than is good for their health. Don't overuse your spouse, either – asking too much of him or her. Share the burden of domestic work between you, especially if you are both working. Both partners must have their rest.

Encourage your spouse to take time out, especially of course on God's Sabbath day of rest. In *Exodus 34:21*, God commanded the Israelites to observe the seventh day for rest. This is reinforced in many other places in the Bible, including the Ten Commandments. Every human being needs rest. Don't wait for your spouse to fall sick before you encourage him or her to take some rest. Tiredness and stress can lead to a nervous breakdown, so you must encourage your spouse to avoid it. If you are deprived of sleep for many days, you can experience serious mental breakdown. The human body needs relaxation.

Thirdly, the body needs exercise to maintain itself in good condition. *1 Timothy 4:8* says that *"bodily exercise profiteth little"* in comparison with godliness, which is *"profitable unto all things"*. Nevertheless, it does profit you a little! Muscles need constant exercise in order to maintain their potential and avoid damage. Exercise stimulates your metabolism, respiration and blood circulation. All these benefit the body. You must encourage your spouse to exercise in order to keep fit. Encourage him or her to find whatever type of exercise suits them best – whether sport, gym work, jogging or whatever.

General fatigue is another enemy that must be dealt with. It could arise from inadequate rest, malnutrition, anaemia, poor posture, emotional tension or habitual lifestyle. Make sure your partner visits your doctor whenever needed. Men especially, can be reluctant to admit their need of medical help.

Due to a lack of adequate provision for body development, many young couples look older than their ages. Your spouse has physical needs that must be met in order for his or her body to develop and function properly.

B. EMOTIONAL DEVELOPMENT

Every human being has emotions. We all feel and react to situations in certain ways depending on our individual emotional maturity and experiences. Your spouse needs you to provide certain things in order to develop a healthy emotional life. Examples of such emotional needs are:

1. Support

You must be supportive to your spouse. You must always be there for him or her. It is your responsibility to support your spouse to achieve his or her dream, vision or plan, so long as it is biblical. You must be actively involved in your spouse's struggle. Never let your spouse do things alone. The essence of marriage is to support each other in all situations. *Ecclesiastes 4:12* illustrates the fact that support gives strength and emotional stability in the face of challenges.

2. Friendship

You must make sure you continue to be a friend to your spouse. In *John 15:14-15*, Jesus calls His disciples friends because He has revealed all His secrets to them. Nothing is hidden. Your spouse needs openness. It will give him or her a sense of security. Let your spouse know everything about you. Put effort into being a friendly person to your spouse. Create a friendly and free atmosphere at home. Don't antagonise your spouse. Don't create a barrier in your relationship. Let there be freedom between you. A person that lives in a friendly environment at home will be friendly outside the home. A hostile environment makes a person unconsciously develop a hostile nature. Also, if you are a friend to your spouse at home, your spouse won't feel so in need of 'someone to talk to' that he or she develops unhealthy relationships with people of the opposite sex outside your home.

3. Encouragement

Your spouse needs encouragement to pass through life and you should be the main provider of it. In the face of any opposition, you must boost your spouse's courage. Help him or her to see light at the end of the tunnel. When people face challenges, they become emotionally unstable, but good words will bring stability. Lift up your partner's spirit. Encourage him or her with the Word of God. This dispels darkness and opens the eye to see beyond the present. Make it a rule that whenever he or she needs a shoulder to cry on, you will be there to help. When your spouse is weak, you must be strong. This quickens emotional restoration.

But encouragement doesn't mean minimising their problems. Put them in the right context of God's plan for our lives, yes, but you must also be able to sympathise with their struggles and appreciate what they are going through. An encourager doesn't encourage by telling someone their problems are small if in reality they are big – that just makes a person feel you don't understand. The Bible teaches us to *"weep with them that weep"* (Romans 12:15). Tears are not a sign of weakness, but a sign that you care.

In 1 Samuel 1:8, Elkanah attempted to encourage his wife, Hannah, who was barren. But how did he go about it? He said: *"Hannah, why weepest thou? And why eatest thou not? And why is thy heart grieved? Am not I better to thee than ten sons?"* This is a classic example of a husband not understanding his wife's feelings. Yes, Hannah loved her husband, but that didn't stop her wanting children. It seems Elkanah was egotistical enough to think that, as long as she had him, how could she need anything else?! He was worth more than ten sons! The fact that Elkanah's words failed to be an encouragement is shown by what follows. In *verse 10*, Hannah is still *"in bitterness of soul, and prayed unto the LORD, and wept sore."*

A person that lives in an atmosphere of discouragement will develop negative emotion towards life, so be an encourager.

4. Empathy

This is the act of showing that you understand someone's feelings (unlike Elkanah, as we saw in 1 Samuel 1:8). It's looking at another person's condition from their perspective. You place yourself in their shoes and feel what they are feeling. Your spouse needs someone who can do this, so you need to learn. Don't laugh when he or she is crying, even if the matter seems trivial to you. It may not be to your spouse. You must realise that people can react differently to the same issue, because they see things differently. In *John 11:33-36*, Jesus wept when he saw Mary and other relatives of Lazarus weeping. Jesus shared their feelings. That is, He brought Himself into their situation. When people saw Jesus weeping in the house of Lazarus, they said Jesus loved Lazarus. Genuine love is sharing the same feeling. Your spouse needs you to share his or her feelings. Empathy creates a sense that someone truly cares about you. A person who lives under such an atmosphere will appreciate love and radiate love.

5. Trust

Your spouse needs to be able to trust you, and know that you trust him or her. They must have confidence in you.

You must build up trust in your spouse. Let him or her see you as a person of integrity. Let your yes be yes and no be no. Trust will make your spouse emotionally stable even in your absence. When an outsider comes to your home to tell a lie against you, it is the trust you have built in your spouse that will speak for you, and he or she will not believe the outsider. In *Genesis 18:19*, God says he knows Abraham and what he is like, so he trusts him. Can your spouse say the same thing about you? When faced with certain issues, your spouse will be emotionally unstable if he or she has no trust in you.

6. Respect

Your spouse needs respect and you must provide it for him or her. Respect will make your spouse feel wanted, accepted and important in the marriage. Respect comes with honour. If you respect your spouse, you will not maltreat him or her and you will not talk badly to him or her. You will always talk nicely to the person you respect. You will never insult those you love if you truly respect them. You will not enter into another relationship if you truly respect your spouse. You will always give honour to him or her and you will not allow other people to disrespect your spouse. You will always protect the person you respect. A person that receives respect at home will develop good self-esteem.

7. Hope

Hebrews 6:19 says that hope is the anchor of the soul. Where there is hope, the spirit is unbreakable. Your spouse must see a future in the marriage. It is your responsibility to create hope in your spouse's mind. Your partner will become anxious and distressed if he or she sees no hope for the marriage in the future. Once your spouse sees no hope in the marriage, selfishness comes in. Such an individual begins to fight for survival with the intention of securing their future. You must make your spouse see that tomorrow will be greater than today, and that it is worth waiting for, or worth working for.

C. MENTAL DEVELOPMENT

For your spouse to grow in mind; the mental self must be developed and this is possible by feeding the mind with good things that will strengthen it. You must encourage your spouse to develop him or herself mentally. In *1 Kings 3:7-9*, Solomon asked for wisdom because he was convinced of his mental limitation.

The journey of mental development begins by identifying the mental limitations of your spouse and encouraging him or her to develop himself or herself accordingly. Support your spouse to improve him or herself academically, and in a chosen career. It will be for the good of the family. Encourage your spouse to reach his or her full potential. But be careful not to push your spouse in a direction or to a level that he or she doesn't want to go – that will only cause stress, anxiety and friction between you, which will be bad for the family.

Also, look out for potential in your spouse. There may be skills or talents that he or she has that could be developed for your spouse's benefit, and for the good of the family. If you identify such a potential, encourage him or her to develop it. It is really enjoyable when we discover we are good at something, and it will improve your spouse's self-esteem.

There is a reason why God deposited such skills in your spouse. It was Joseph's skill that opened the door to greatness for him (*Genesis 41:39-40*). It was David's skill that brought him into the presence of the king (*1 Samuel 16:18-19*). There are many homes that remain stagnant because of in-house rivalry between the couples. Instead of encouraging each other to develop the skills God has deposited in them for the advancement of their home, they resort to jealousy and unhealthy competition.

Create an atmosphere at home where the mind of everybody in the family will be filled with good thoughts and creative ideas. This helps to develop the mind. Some people have become mental midgets because their minds are continually being filled with strife, arguments, accusations and insults. What a waste of brain power! Good ideas will only come from a settled, stress-free mind. Make your home a place of peace, where everyone can learn good things.

It also doesn't help a family to spend a lot of time watching TV programmes where strife and envy are the constant themes. This is often true of soap operas like East Enders, Emmerdale and Coronation Street, where ungodly patterns of behaviour are constantly presented, but virtually any secular programme or movie can be a negative influence on the mind. If you are parents, you should be careful to control what your children watch and which games they play. Excessive use of computer games or too much of any form of secular entertainment can be bad for our mind

– filling it with words and concepts that are contrary to God's kingdom. We all need times of relaxation, and there's nothing wrong with being entertained, but for healthy mental development, we do need to fill our minds with good things, as *Philippians 4:8* teaches.

D. SPIRITUAL DEVELOPMENT

Your spouse needs you for spiritual growth. Encourage your spouse to learn how to take all things to God in prayer. Build the faith of your spouse in God. Let your spouse see in you the attitude of faith. Be sure to challenge every negative confession your spouse makes. Help him or her to cultivate the habit of speaking words of faith instead. Have a prayer altar at home and develop a workable plan for regular prayer together. Study the word of God together and let your spouse play a role in the sharing of the word of God. Make space and time for your spouse to serve God.

Deciding which church to join can be crucial in a couple's spiritual development. Pray together as a couple to make this decision, which should be based on the spiritual needs that every Christian has. These include: sound teaching from the Word of God; fervent prayer; regular spiritual exercise; a strong sense of holiness and righteousness, and the manifestation of the love of God. This is the kind of church that will help your home to grow spiritually.

After inner conviction, encourage your spouse to work for God in a certain capacity, and let him or her see your dedication to the things of God. Gradually, you will build a home that fears God. Unless there is the fear of God planted in both you and your spouse, it is a matter of time before disaster happens. A wild animal is far less dangerous to you than a person who does not fear God. Your life is not safe in the hands of such a person. Make the Word of God the final authority in your home. Let your spouse see that you surrender to the dictates of the Word of God, and he or she will follow suit naturally. When you encourage your spouse to get closer to God and both of you attend a Bible-based church, positive changes will happens at home.

Chapter Four

PLANS TO CONSIDER

Home is about management with purpose. Every home is blessed with human beings, material resources and every good thing that will make the home fulfilled. All these resources need effective management and wise usage. This will determine the future of the home. Therefore, it is the responsibility of the couple to plan how they will run their home, if they are to have a fulfilled life.

Advantages of having plans for your home include: effective channelling of resources and actions towards a beneficial purpose; a clear understanding of where you are going in life and evaluation of progress, and identification of your strengths, weaknesses, identity and opportunities. A home plan will also enable you to know how to handle threats to your home's vision. All these will determine what you will become in life.

Your plans for your home must include the following:

1. GROWTH

Effective management of your body, soul and spirit will determine the level of your growth as a human being.

You must have plans for how individual members of your home will develop physically, emotionally and spiritually. This has been covered in chapter 3.

2. SOCIAL DEVELOPMENT

You must have plans for the social development of your family. Make sure you plan times of relaxation, visits to friends and relatives and other social activities into your schedule. Social interaction will exercise your brain and help you to regularly see new things that will stimulate your thinking. Through social development, you will improve your ability to relate to people, whatever their gender, culture or religion. Relating with outsiders will also give you insight into how other families live and help you to discover new ideas you can take back to your home, to improve it in some areas. There is a lot to learn from your environment and people around you.

Exposure to life outside your home will help you to realise that there are certain things common to all homes, irrespective of gender or family background. You will soon discover that your spouse is not the worst person on earth! You will also discover that things are not as bad in your home as you previously thought. When you are able to observe situations outside your home, you will have every reason to thank God for your marriage.

So, develop a plan for a good social life and help your family members to develop good self-esteem through interaction with the bigger world. Your social life can help you to improve your character and develop good ways to relate to other people. This will influence your relationship with your spouse. There are good homes and successful people around you. Talk to those who have successful marriages and you will learn a lot from them. Make friends with God-fearing people. They will teach you how to relate with your spouse in the fear of God.

3. FAMILY SIZE

You must include in your plan the size of the family you want. The result is not entirely in your hands, of course, as there are natural factors that can affect fertility. So your plans may not come to fruition, but it is still responsible to make what plans you can. Be prayerful about your decision, and come to an agreement between you. How many children do you want to have? This may be affected by the nature of careers and the resources available. If your career involves travelling from place to place, it means you will not always be at home to share the burden of parenting. It will be a mistake to have many children if they will not enjoy parental support. Your children must witness their parents living together so that they can learn how to live with their own spouses in the future.

Also, if you live in a country where there is no financial support for the family to bring up their children, it means that you and your spouse will be totally responsible for the cost of your children's upbringing. It would therefore be wise not to have more children than you can cater for. Parenting is expensive and demanding. Don't produce children you can't train because untrained children will grow up to have chaotic and, most probably, immoral lives. They may even become criminals, destroying the lives of innocent people. Many children who grow up to become criminals and murderers that kill bread-winners of innocent families come from unstable families. A lack of good parenting can have serious consequences.

You have not finished parenting your child until the child can live independently (and even then they will continue to need your advice and help). This actually takes time.

4. WEALTH CREATION

"A good man leaveth an inheritance to his children's children: and the wealth of the sinner is laid up for the just." **Proverbs 13:22**

If you don't want to die poor and live your entire life under financial pressure, you need to have a plan for how your home can create more wealth. It requires financial freedom to run a home and empower every family member to be fulfilled. Wealth creation involves spending wisely, investing well, acquiring assets and having savings.

Ideally, your home should have more than one source of income. The reason not to have 'all your eggs in one basket' is that jobs these days are rarely jobs for life – they can be insecure – and business investments can fail. So having more than one source of money frees your home from financial uncertainty. If one source of making money becomes weak or comes to an end, the other sources will keep your home going.

You should have an investment plan, to make more money than just your salary. Most salaries are not big enough to make anybody wealthy; they only make you comfortable. Your home must find a new way of making money. Proverbs teaches that it is good to leave an inheritance for your children's children. This can only be possible if you have investments and assets.

There is a lot of potential in you that you can exploit to make your family life better. There are so many investment opportunities around that you can get involved in to make more money for your home. Money can grow, but you must create a plan to make it happen – it won't grow in a normal bank account. You can buy shares in big companies. You can start a small business, and with God on your side, it is a matter of time; it will grow. Gradually, you can free your home from financial pressure. But as you must be a good steward of the financial blessings God has given you – don't take big risks with your investments. Do all you can to ensure you are investing wisely. Seek the help of a trusted Christian financial advisor if you need to.

5. FINANCIAL RETENTION

Having more than enough money coming into the home is one thing; retaining money at home is another. In order to avoid wastage, you must have a savings plan and you must avoid unnecessary spending. Saving is needed to make money grow. A certain percentage of money coming into your home should be put into savings, to cater for future needs and to build up a fund for investments. Many families live from pay cheque to pay cheque. They move round the cycle of financial insufficiency. Unless you have a plan to adhere to, you will find it hard to retain money.

Financial discipline is needed to avoid waste. Don't be stingy to your spouse, children and yourself, but also, don't be wasteful.

6. CAREER

You must have a plan for both of your careers. You must agree to help each other develop your careers. Spend time planning how each of you will further your education for career development. This should be done without putting your family under immense pressure that can lead to crisis. It is important to note that career development is for both spouses. There will be imbalance in the way the home is being run if only one spouse develops his or her career. It puts the family finances at greater risk if there is only one income, because there will be nothing to fall back on if there is any challenge facing the career and the job of the person that developed his or her career. Where do you want you and your spouse to be in your careers in the next five, ten or fifteen years? Make the plan now, including career breaks that may be necessary in order to bring up children – especially when they are young. But be flexible with your plan in the future – your ideas may have to change, depending on circumstances.

7. VALUES TO LIVE FOR

Your home must have values to live by. Values are your personal beliefs and ideals on moral and ethical issues, and your opinions on what is good or bad and desirable or undesirable. They should be shared by all the members of your family, and of course they should be drawn from a good understanding of Bible teaching. Your values influence your behaviour and attitude, and serve as broad guidelines to you in all situations.

For example, you can make it a tradition in your home that your family will always eat together. This contributes to relational development in the family. Let it also be a value in your home that your family will never miss church services. Also, your values must include observing a daily prayer altar where the family come together to pray and share the Word of God.

Also, you must make it part of your family values that you and your spouse will never insult each other, no matter the level of disagreement. It would also be good to agree in your home that you and your spouse will never go to bed until every disagreement of the day is sorted out. That is, you will not go to bed annoyed with each other (see *Ephesians 4:26*).

Generally, values in Christian homes involve honesty, integrity, respect, godliness, serving God, and other God-fearing behaviours. Your values must show commitment to marriage. You must also project a good family image to outsiders. Never be angry with your spouse in public. You must always honour each other, because you are setting an example to others and being an ambassador of Christ – both inside and outside the home.

8. MISSION

Develop a mission statement for your family that you and your spouse will commit to pursuing. Mission is a statement of direction and purpose. There must be strategies on how to achieve the mission. You and your spouse must devote your lives to the achievement of the purpose. First, there is the individual purpose – the vision you have developed individually, probably before marriage. Your individual visions must be harmonized to form a common purpose for the marriage.

Similarly, there must be a purpose towards each other. This is the reason why you married each other. Obviously, your purpose is to love each other and any children you may have, but each individual also has an assignment to carry out in another person's life, to glorify God's name. That is why it is important for each of you to know why you have married each other. There must be a reason why God has brought you together to marry each other. This purpose must be established from the outset. You must know why you married the person you have married.

Where there is lack of purpose, confusion and conflict is inevitable. Some people marry in order to assist each other to grow closer to Christ individually, while some marry to fulfil their ministry to others. Some marry to bring the light of God into the rest of the family of the spouse. God allows marriage for good reasons, which may be specific or general, and there may be more than one purpose. But both of you have a responsibility to discover the purpose or purposes of your marriage.

All these will form your home mission statement.

9. GOALS

A goal is an end. It is what you will become in future. Goals will dictate to you how to direct and channel your resources and energy. Your home must have goals which must be developed spiritually. You must have goals for your children, i.e. what do you want your children to become in future? (This is not necessarily about career choice, as that will be their choice in the end, but this is more about their character, morals and spiritual development.) You must have goals for your spouse, i.e. what do you want your spouse to become in future? There must be a personal goal too – what you want to become in future. If you fail to develop a goal, your home will not have direction. Your goals must encompass every segment of your life, such as spouse, self, children, career, children's education, level of education for children to attain, etc. What level of knowledge do you want every member of your family to attain in God? This is a goal. This is what you, your spouse and children will become in future. Develop plans to achieve them. Of course, not all goals are reached, especially if you set your targets too high, but if you don't have goals you won't achieve anything.

10. PEOPLE TO JOURNEY WITH YOU

Your family will always need people to journey with in life, but you must choose them wisely. People to live with include friends and relatives. You must put people into different categories and determine the level of their closeness to your family. Irrespective of the level of relationship, not everybody is qualified to know all the details of your marriage. Don't sell your home out. Don't expose your marriage to just anybody. Some people should not know your family secrets. You must set boundaries for people around you when it comes to your marital issues. Generally, people you have not tested should not be trusted with certain information about your marriage.

Don't expose your spouse to avoidable attacks. You must know that people around you will change towards you as situations in your home change. When God begins to move your home from success to success, there are people around you who will not be able to accommodate it. Such people become envious, and this makes them suitable to be used by the devil for any evil assignment. It is your responsibility to identify such people from the outset and put them where they belong in your life. Some people are naturally rebellious and they criticise every good thing, especially if they won't benefit from that particular thing. This makes them suitable to be used to betray people. For anybody to qualify to be a close associate of your family, the person must be a Christian of proven integrity. You must be perceptive about a person's character. You must know that backbiters and gossips destroy relationships. Also, a friend or relative that does not fear God will not be afraid to destroy your home, if given reason to. Don't be deceived by untested loyalty.

11. COUNSELLOR

There will be a time in your marriage that you will need somebody to show you and your spouse the way to go in certain issues of your relationship. You will always need an adviser and counsellor. The person you choose as counsellor will determine your decisions in many situations. It is therefore necessary that your counsellor meets certain requirements. Such requirements are:

a. **Experience.** Your counsellor must be an individual who has been married for at least five years. It is impossible to give out what you don't have. A person who has not married will only give you advice he or she has not tested. It will be theoretical advice and what you need is something practical.

b. **Success.** Your counsellor must have a record of a successful marriage. He or she must not be a divorcee. There must be evidence that he or she has successfully practised the marriage principles he or she wants to share with you.

c. **Christian faith.** Your counsellor must be a Christian, preferably with evidence of a close relationship with God. You must know that people talk according to their deeply held beliefs and principles. An unbeliever will offer you worldly counsel and will lead your home into future crisis. Don't choose counsellors outside the kingdom of God.

d. **Independence.** Your counsellor must not be a close relation to you, such as a parent or uncle. Though well meaning, close relatives tend to be sentimental and not real. They usually take sides and give counsel under emotion. Prayerfully choose a counsellor that is not a blood relation to either you or your spouse. Find a person who holds a position of honour in the house of

God, or a mature elder who is Spirit–filled. The general condition every counsel you receive must meet is that it fits with the Word of God. Counsel that is contrary to God's Word will lead your home into crisis, and it shall not receive the blessings of God.

12. PARENTING

This concerns the way you and your spouse will train your children. There must be an agreement between you about the type of strategies you will employ in parenting. Generally, you and your spouse must avoid the following:

a. **Arguing in front of the children.** Never disagree between yourselves in the presence of your children about methods of parenting. If you do, you will send a message to your children that there is vulnerability between you and your spouse and the children will exploit it.

b. **Favouritism.** Never make your child develop a feeling that either you or your spouse has a stronger sentiment towards him or her. Don't let your child feel that he or she is loved better by one or the other of you. Such a child will consider the parent he or she believes does not love them so much as an enemy, and so develop resentment towards such a parent.

c. **Disagreement in front of the children.** Never correct the parenting style of your spouse within hearing distance of your children. If you do, it will give the child a wrong mind-set that he or she is being treated unfairly by the parent who is being corrected.

d. **Apparent disunity.** Never let your child know which of the parents used money to buy him or her certain goods. Let your child know that it is the family money that is being used for him or her, not yours personally. Avoid passing the message of individualism to your child. Don't let the child think he or she is more loved by either of the parents because one of them is always spending money on them or spends more time with them. Never take sides with your child against your spouse.

13. FAMILY IMAGE

You must decide from the beginning the kind of image you want to project to the public and your in-laws. Examples of such images are:

a. **Letting people know that you love each other.** Avoid giving bad reports about your spouse to people – especially your in-laws. If you speak badly about your spouse to outsiders, it is an indication that you don't love each other, and when people sense this they will start sowing evil seeds into your home, directly and indirectly. Avoid going to your in-laws to complain about your spouse. It will create fear in the minds of your in-laws that their child is not in safe hands. Avoid giving your own parents bad impressions of your spouse. It will make them develop negative feelings towards your spouse. The consequences of this may be beyond your control.

b. **Letting people know that there is unity in your marriage.** Never argue with your spouse publicly. It will send the bad message to people that there is disunity in your marriage. If you think there is an issue in your marriage and you need help, seek help instead of advertising your home wrongly to the outsider.

c. **Letting people know that you are capable of handling marriage.** You must project wisdom in public. Incessant complaints about your home to other people are an indication that you lack the wisdom necessary to manage your home. People will soon start coming to you, stating that they want to help you. But it means they don't have respect for your abilities as a married person.

d. **Letting people know that you respect your spouse.** Demonstrate this outside. Honour your spouse outside. This will determine how people treat your spouse. If they respect your spouse, they will also respect your home.

e. **Training your children not to broadcast bad news about your home to outsiders.** Teach them to keep family secrets secret. What other children hear from your children is what they will tell their parents at home. That is why you must limit the level of information your children will have access to at home. Children can't handle certain information due to their age. Don't be careless in front of your children.

f. **Letting people know that your home is a Christian home and you are not ready to compromise.** Project this image as early as possible. When people know that your home is a Christian home, they will not expect certain things from you and your spouse. Let your parents and in-laws know that your home is a Christian home. This will most likely prevent them from inviting you to join in family traditions that may not be appropriate for a Christian. It will also hopefully stop them from seeking help for you from wrong sources, such as New Age gurus, occultists or witch doctors. Let them know what your home stands for.

g. **Letting people know that you are a married person.** Don't hide your marital status. There are certain things a married person should not get involved in. For example, you are not supposed to have a close relationship with someone of the opposite sex, though; there may be no intention of marital unfaithfulness. It will be a sign of lack of respect to your spouse if you get too close to someone outside your marriage. It will open the door to temptation. So, don't visit a person of the opposite sex alone. Your spouse must accompany you, or at least another friend. In all your decisions outside the home, such as at your work place, you must put your home first. Don't visit friends after working hours till late without your spouse's approval. It is a sign of lack of respect to your partner. If people see you spending a lot of time without your spouse, they will begin to think that maybe you don't enjoy being at home with your spouse, and they will gossip this to others. It is the wrong image to send out to others. Don't be careless with your marriage.

14. CRISIS MANAGEMENT

Nobody prays for crises, but nevertheless they will come! We pass through different stages in life and we should know how to handle them as we find ourselves caught up in them. You must have a plan for how to manage a crisis, such as misunderstandings. How do you handle arguments? What method will you adopt to deal with certain ugly situations? Agree with your spouse that it will be a family rule never to engage in strife, no matter the seriousness of the matter. You must always allow the peace of God to reign in your home in all situations, because without peace, there is no solution that can work.

Get rid of fear and anxiety. This will create good ground for the Holy Spirit to help your home in your crisis. In a Christian home, the first method is prayer. You must pray together for God to enlighten your understanding, so as to adopt the right course of action. You must study the Bible with an intention that God will speak to you as an individual concerning the matter at home. You must have family discussion over the matter, because God can decide to speak through any of you.

If no solution seems forthcoming, then take a break from it for a few days and later come back to the issue. This will allow each of you to have a personal encounter with God over the matter. If there is still no solution, you should consult your spiritual father in the Lord – your pastor or your counsellor.

In it all, you should ask God to confirm whether your way of dealing with the crisis is of Him. If it is of God, you will receive peace from God over the matter. The solution will also agree with the Word of God.

Chapter Five

THE FIRST LOVE

This was the love that existed between you and your spouse at the beginning of your relationship. At that early stage, both of you came into the relationship innocently and without any prejudice. You had pure hearts towards each other and all your actions were pure and without blemish. The first love is always the best love between couples. How wonderful it would be if the first love can be maintained in the relationship.

> *"Nevertheless I have somewhat against thee, because thou hast left thy first love."* **Revelation 2:4**

The church in Ephesus left their first love towards God. Qualities of this first love are:

1. FERVOUR

Actions done under the first love is hot, glowing and fervent. Everyone around will notice that you love the person you claim to love. It will be difficult for you to hide the fact that you are in love. It is very intense. Without being told, people around will notice that the two of you love each other. You carry each other's bags, help each other publicly, hold hands, gaze into each other's eyes when talking, etc. You don't feel shy. You may even carry a photo of the person around. This sends a clear signal out to the world that you are not available for a close relationship with any other person because you are already committed to someone.

2. CHEERFULNESS

Actions done under the first love are filled with joy and laughter. You are always radiating joy whenever you are together. You are always willing to please your lover. You don't even notice the faults of the other person. Even your voice is tender towards each other. His or her presence around you gives you confidence and joy. You love being around each other.

3. WILLINGNESS

Your heart and mind is focused on pleasing your partner and you are willing to do anything for them. There is no reluctance in you towards the person. Under the first love, if your partner calls you once, you answer twice, because your mind is always turned towards him or her. You are always ready to do the will of the other person.

4. ZEAL

Actions done under the first love are filled with zeal. You are passionate about the person you love. You have an undivided interest in them, and are always thinking about him or her. You are ready to pay any sacrifice and take any risk to please the person you love. Under the first love everything is possible because you are ready to deny yourself of any benefit in order to help your lover. Where there is a will, there is always a way.

5. WHOLEHEARTEDNESS

Under the first love, whatever you do, you do it heartily. All your actions are done with devotion and full concentration. You are thorough and complete. You please each other with all your might and the totality of yourself. There is no division of heart. There is no hesitation in your actions. You are real and genuine. No pretence. There is dedication.

6. HASTE

Actions done under the first love are done in haste (which sometimes isn't wise, but it shows your love). There is no waste of time. There is speed in action. With the first love, there is no procrastination of action. Your attitude is good and encouraging, without hesitation.

7. PERFECTION

Love is blind! Under the first love, your actions are flawless and you see no flaw in your lover. You don't do each other wrong because you don't want to hurt each other. Your lover is always right under the first love. This is the time you demonstrate that love truly can cover a multitude of sins.

Finally, it is only under the first love that you can really put *1 Corinthians 13* into practice.

THE LOSS OF FIRST LOVE

Our first love can be lost. As the relationship develops, unfortunately certain wrong things start coming into the relationship. These begin to strain the relationship and the fire of love starts to cool. Unknowingly, couples start pointing fingers and enter into the blame game. If unchecked, this turns the home into a war zone where there is incessant strife and conflict.

The causes of this loss of love are:

1. Imbalance

If love is not reciprocated and only one person is making an effort to make it work, discouragement sets in. To maintain sincere love in a relationship, there must be a balance. Each party must make an effort to work things out. Keeping the first love is the responsibility of both partners.

2. Divided heart

If you share your heart with another person, your commitment towards your partner will reduce and the first love will disappear. A divided heart could be due to adultery. You can't maintain the first love in a relationship when your heart is shared with another person. Similarly, a divided heart could be due to wrong attachment to a friend or relative. If you allow another person to occupy the position that only your spouse should occupy, the first love will diminish. If you give too much regard to a person or you have a confidant who is not your spouse, your heart will be divided. Your spouse should be number one in your life, after God.

3. Relaxation

If you stop doing the right things that you used to do at the beginning of the relationship, the first love will start going down. Love needs effort and consistency. You have to work things out. You have to be consistent in good habits. You should not stop doing what gives your spouse joy. If you slack in your relationship, you will give room for suspicions.

4. Familiarity

Familiarity makes you take each other for granted. After marriage, you and your spouse live together and see each other frequently. Soon you get used to each other and start seeing each other's faults and weaknesses. Unconsciously, you start losing respect for each other and also lose a sense of importance towards each other. This will affect your first love. Avoid taking your partner for granted. Never lose respect for your spouse. Ensure that you remember that you need each other in life.

5. Distractions

These are situations the enemy will create in your relationship to shift your attention from the initial promises you made towards each other at the beginning of the relationship. You have pledged at the beginning that you will always cherish each other and that you will never hurt each other. Gradually, the enemy starts to create situations that will generate blame, disagreement, accusations, fault-findings, etc. All these will make your love grow cold, if you allow it.

6. **Stagnancy**

Anything that does not grow will soon die. To maintain the first love, it must grow. Love that will last must increase. You must love more. You must give more. You must be kind more. You must increase in tolerance. You must increase in humility. You must do more good. Don't be stagnant in love.

7. **Availability**

If love is to endure, you need to spend time together. If you don't spend time with God, your love towards God will diminish. If you get so busy that you don't have time for your spouse, your absence will create a vacuum, and raise questions that your partner will not be able to answer. Love is about sharing hearts together and communicating with each other. Your spouse needs your presence; otherwise the first love will start dying.

8. **Another voice**

When you begin to listen to another voice apart from that of your spouse, the first love starts decreasing. Whoever you listen to will influence your thoughts and actions. Don't harbour every word you hear in your heart. The only word that you should allow to influence your thoughts in any decision that affects your marriage is the word of your spouse. Only your spouse understands your feelings. Only your spouse truly cares about your well-being, because whatever affects you automatically affects your spouse. If your decision-making is more influenced by what an outsider has told you than what your partner says, you will undermine the first love in your spouse's heart.

9. Looking backwards

Relationships will last if those involved are always looking forward. You must look forward for the good days ahead of you. If you look backwards, thinking those old days are better than the present days, you will begin to see your spouse as the root cause of your stagnation. Love will start to grow cold. You must always be thankful for marrying the person you have married, whatever the situation. You don't know what might have happened if you had married someone else. You might have married a worse person than your present spouse. Just thank God and stop thinking about what you don't know. Don't look backwards. Don't look into the offence of yesterday. Look forward in your relationship. Be hopeful that there is a better future. Be a person of hope.

10. Pressures of life

The pressures we all live under can make you conform to the dictates of life that will not please your spouse. Due to these pressures, you may make certain decisions that are to the detriment of your spouse, or lose your original purpose, vision or integrity. Your spouse begins to see a person who is different from the one he or she married some years ago. If you surrender to the pressures of life, your spouse may not like the person you have become. You may fall into deception, manipulation, insincerity and every manner of strange behaviour. If your spouse didn't see any of these characteristics in you at the beginning of your relationship, he or she may start doubting your reliability and worry about the future of your relationship. Your spouse wants to continue to see in you those good attributes seen in you at the beginning of the relationship. The first love can dwindle if you *"let the world around you squeeze you into its own mould"* (Romans 12:2).

11. Disappointments

Many people come into marriage with a lot of unrealistic expectations, so when their marriage fails to live up to those expectations they start losing interest in the relationship. Many people expect that marriage will improve their lives, but have never thought how that would happen. They naively assume that married life will be some kind of paradise for them. They may even notice their marriage partner's faults before the wedding, but still believe that after the wedding, things will be different. Unfortunately, the fiancé or fiancée does not turn into some kind of angel after marriage. The partner will soon discover that they were wrong. This disillusionment results in loss of the first love. If you no longer love your spouse as before, you may need to check what brought you into the relationship in the beginning.

12. New discoveries

After marriage, there are always surprises! It's only after living together for some time that you discover more of your partner's faults. You may find that your spouse covered up certain areas of his or her life to prevent you from knowing the truth, but now the truth has come out. You may also discover some damaging truths about your spouse that he or she was not aware of. Sometimes it takes others to see failings and point them out. Some of these discoveries could undermine your initial trust in the person you have married. Perhaps you would not have married this person if you had known about certain behaviours or facts in the beginning. If you don't prayerfully handle the matter, you may lose your first love and even start hating your spouse. You must understand that whether God wanted you to marry this person or not, He knows how to work the problem out. For God to have allowed you to marry each other, He must have put some good plans in place for your future, because *"we know that all things work together for good to them that love God"* (Romans 8:28). Therefore, stay in the relationship. You may not have known the hidden things at the beginning of your relationship, but your God knew. Surrender it all to the all- knowing God.

13. Childishness

Nothing is secure in the hand of a child. You must grow into maturity in your relationship. After marriage, more maturity will be needed from your side to cope with all the new events you will face. You will need more maturity than you had before marrying, in order to relate well to the relatives of your spouse, to tolerate unexpected situations, and to avoid over-reacting to situations at home. If you refuse to grow morally and spiritually, you will create a negative environment in your marriage. A childish spouse can't maintain the first love because he or she does not even recognise its importance due to immaturity. Without maturity, the first love will come under serious attack.

14. Ignorance

After marriage, situations around you and your spouse will change significantly. For example, because you are spending more time together, you will find that you both have less time for your previous circle of friends. This can result in gradual loss of some friendships, and regret on behalf of one or both of the partners. If you don't anticipate this change and understand it is a natural part of your commitment in marriage, then one or the other of you may grow to resent the effect of your marriage on your life. You must be able to interpret changes correctly, if you are to avoid costly errors. Due to lack of understanding, you may take some situations personally and react wrongly. This may attract anger from your spouse, and if the situation is not quickly resolved, suspicions and worry may set in. You must deal with your spouse with understanding in order to avoid unhelpful reactions.

15. Incessant disagreement

It is impossible for two people to walk together without agreement on major issues. Disagreement breeds disunity and creates room for unnecessary suspicion in a relationship. If you and your spouse always engage in disagreement over every matter, it is only a matter of time; the first love will begin to dissolve. Disagreement leads to rejection. You will start avoiding each other when it comes to certain issues that affect your home. This can lead to individualism, a situation whereby an individual starts operating alone and pursues his or her individual agenda. To maintain the first love, you must ensure that you reach agreement over issues of life. You must also accept that there are always going to be minor things that you disagree on. But you must agree to disagree agreeably, and move on! Don't let small disagreements grow into larger arguments.

There must be give and take – don't think you have to win every argument. If you try to get your own way all the time, you will certainly destroy that first love. You can win an argument and lose a relationship. Be prepared to make sacrifices in order to maintain your marriage.

16. Lawlessness

This is living in certain sins. It is a continual act of disobedience to God's rules. Sins make you ignore the boundary between good and evil, and your actions will start to attract the devil into the affairs of your home. Wherever there is sin, Satan is present. Satan generates hatred. To maintain the first love, avoid practising sins. Repent quickly and ask God for forgiveness, and for His help to overcome any sins you struggle with.

HOW TO MAINTAIN THE FIRST LOVE

"Remember therefore from whence thou art fallen, and repent, and do the first works; or else I will come unto thee quickly, and will remove thy candlestick out of his place, except thou repent." **Revelation 2:5**

To maintain the first love is to continue to do the first works – the things you did to please each other at the beginning. Keep up those good works – and improve on them! Don't stop doing what you have been doing since the beginning of the relationship. Keep on cherishing each other, as you did before marriage. Keep on putting your partner before yourself. Keep up the romance. Take your stand against all that seeks to undermine your marriage, not allowing changing situations around you to damage your love for each other.

> *"But Jesus beheld them, and said unto them, With men this is impossible; but with God all things are possible."*
> **Matthew 19:26**

We all change as time goes on – our personalities change, our needs change, and our opinions change. For this reason it is inevitable that each partner has to understand and accept that change does happen. Hopefully there will be more significant changes for the better than for the worse! But because we change, you will need God to remain constant in your relationship. Prayerfully commit your relationship into the hands of God, because with Him all things really are possible!

> *"Except the LORD build the house, they labour in vain that build it: except the LORD keep the city, the watchman waketh but in vain."* **Psalm 127:1**

Let God take central place in your home and encourage each other to fear God. With God as the builder of your home, you will notice that you love each other more and more as the days pass by. It is possible to maintain the first love with God on your side.

Don't forget to remind each other about the beginning of your relationship. Whenever you notice negative changes, either from you or your spouse, remind each other about the beginning. Remember how you used to treat each other in the beginning and encourage each other to return to the beginning. Return to the old good days when you saw each other as an angel without fault. Return to the good old days when your spouse was always right in your sight. Return to the good old days when you could not do without each other. Abandon any wrong behaviour that may drive a wedge between you.

Chapter Six

THE STRAWS OF MARRIAGE

> *"Ye shall no more give the people straw to make brick, as heretofore: let them go and gather straw for themselves."*
> ***Exodus 5:7***

The Israelites worked for the Egyptians. They used clay bricks to build houses for the Egyptians.

Straw – the dried stalks of cereal plants – was mixed with the clay to make the bricks more firm and durable. Without straw, the bricks would crumble and break. Each individual stalk in a brick helped to hold it together.

To keep your marriage together, you will need certain straws. As long as these straws are present in your home, no devil can break up your home. With these straws in your relationship, you will overcome every manner of challenges and your home will always bounce back after a major challenge.

The five major straws that keep home together in all situations are:

1. LOVE

What is love? *1 John 4:8* says: *"He that loveth not knoweth not God; for God is love."*

Love is God. When you claim to love your spouse, it means that you are revealing the nature of God to your spouse. This implies that it is impossible to love without God. Where there is love, there is God. If you want to know how to love your spouse, try to understand how God shows love to His people. If you bring this kind of love into your marriage, nothing will be able to destroy it.

How does God love?

a. He loves with action

> *"For God so loved the world, that he gave his only begotten Son, that whosoever believeth in him should not perish, but have everlasting life."* **John 3:16**

The love of God towards man prompted Him to act in love by giving the only Son He has to redeem mankind. If you truly love your spouse, you will back it up with an action of love. Given the choice between saving your own life and saving your spouse's, you will choose your spouse. You will be ready to do whatever you can do to please the person you love, otherwise you are not in love.

b. He loves unchangeably

> *"For I am the LORD, I change not; therefore ye sons of Jacob are not consumed."* **Malachi 3:6**

God loves His people today just as much as He did yesterday. Genuine love does not depreciate but appreciate. You are not supposed to give up treating your spouse well, whatever the situation. You must keep on loving your spouse whether you become rich or poor. You must keep on loving your spouse in both good times and bad. You must keep on loving your spouse whether he or she still loves you or hates you. Even when children of God practise evil, God still loves them. You should not stop loving, even when your spouse stops loving you.

If you keep showing love to your spouse even if he or she no longer loves you, it is just a matter of time before your love wins him or her over to your side. Love never gives up. Love is spiritual because God who is love is also spiritual. A woman refused to remarry after her husband went with another woman. After many years, the man came back home. The love of the wife won him over. This was possible because the woman refused to stop loving the man, though the man had stopped loving her. As long as one of the parties in marriage refuses to stop loving, the covenant of marriage will remain, and may bring the runaway partner home.

c. **He loves with constraint**

> *"I drew them with cords of a man, with bands of love: and I was to them as they that take off the yoke on their jaws, and I laid meat unto them."* **Hosea 11:4**

Love constrains God not to treat mankind as he deserves. Due to His love for people, when someone deserves to be cast away, God will resist that temptation. If you truly love your spouse, you will not let his or her bad behaviour influence you to act in a bad way. You will not treat him or her badly, despite the fact that your spouse deserves punishment for a sinful action. Love constrains. Love is not quick to punish, and neither does it pay evil for evil. Let your love towards your spouse constrain you from doing evil to him or her, irrespective of the evil he or she might have done to you.

d. He loves rigidly

> *"For I am persuaded, that neither death, nor life, nor angels, nor principalities, nor powers, nor things present, nor things to come, nor height, nor depth, nor any other creature, shall be able to separate us from the love of God, which is in Christ Jesus our Lord."* **Romans 8:38-39**

The cord of the love of God is unbreakable. There is nothing that can separate you from His love. If you love your spouse with the love of God, you will always love him or her in all situations. If nothing can separate your spouse from your love towards him or her, it means your home will be unbreakable. Whatever the enemy may do to destroy your relationship, he will fail – because the cord of love in your relationship is unbreakable.

e. He loves with understanding

> *"As far as the east is from the west, so far hath he removed our transgressions from us. Like as a father pitieth his children, so the LORD pitieth them that fear him. For he knoweth our frame; he remembereth that we are dust."*
> **Psalm 103:12-14**

God is God and He has not created another God like himself. He is the only one who can never fail. In all His dealings with His children, He constantly remembers their origin. God knows that nothing which comes from the dust is perfect. If you truly love your spouse, you will deal with him or her with understanding. You must understand that your spouse is different from you. You must know that your spouse is not as strong as you are in all things. Your spouse is weak where you are strong and vice versa. Therefore, you must control your expectations from your spouse. Your spouse will not always satisfy you. He or she is not God. There will be times of disappointment when you thought he or she was supposed to do better. Your spouse is not you and you are not your spouse. There are inherent differences between the two of you and these will affect how individuals function under various situations. It is a human being you have married, not an angel. Congratulations to you if you have abundant grace to function well under various situations, but remember it is not the same with everybody.

f. He loves deeply

> *"For thus saith the LORD of hosts; After the glory hath he sent me unto the nations which spoiled you: for he that toucheth you toucheth the apple of his eye."*
> **Zechariah 2:8**

When the children of God are sad, God is also sad. When God's children are in the fire, God is in the fire with them. He feels their pain. If you love your spouse genuinely with God's type of love, whatever touches him or her automatically touches you. You always feel the pain of your spouse. For that reason, you will not want anything to cause him or her pain. You will not subject your spouse to pain because you will indirectly put yourself in pain. This makes you always protect your spouse against any attack or discomfort.

g. He loves to eternity

> *"Behold, for peace I had great bitterness: but thou hast in love to my soul delivered it from the pit of corruption: for thou hast cast all my sins behind thy back."* **Isaiah 38:17**

God loves you and cares a lot about your soul. He wants to see all His children in eternity. If you genuinely love your spouse, you will care about his or her soul. You will encourage your spouse to come closer to God. You will show him or her the love of God to draw him or her to God.

With the love of God, your home will always remain intact in all difficulties. This straw sustains the home in all situations that are designed to break and deform it.

2. OBEDIENCE

Obedience to God is another straw that holds homes together. To obey means to follow instructions in totality. Your actions as a married person affect not only you but everyone in your home (children and your spouse). You will do your home immense good if you obey God in all your ways. Through your obedience to God, you will make today and tomorrow better for your home.

In *Joshua 7:24-26* it was Achan who sinned, but the whole of his family perished. Disobedience to God will put your home in danger. Continual disobedience to God will expose your home to danger and disintegration. In *2 Samuel 12:15-18* it was David who sinned, but it was his child that died as a punishment for his sin. Sin will endanger all your family members.

Some of the punishments that have been ordained for the family members of a disobedient person are shown in the Bible verses below:

Job 27:13-14 says: *"This is the portion of a wicked man with God, and the heritage of oppressors, which they shall receive of the Almighty. If his children be multiplied, it is for the sword: and his offspring shall not be satisfied with bread."* That is, the family of a disobedient person is under the curse of continual hardship. Hardship has contributed to the disintegration of many homes.

Deuteronomy 28:15 & 41 says: *"But it shall come to pass, if thou wilt not hearken unto the voice of the Lord thy God, to observe to do all his commandments and his statutes which I command thee this day; that all these curses shall come upon thee… Thou shalt beget sons and daughters, but thou shalt not enjoy them; for they shall go into captivity."*

These verses show that the children of a disobedient person will be oppressed. This is one of the curses that disobedience brings upon the family of a disobedient person.

Psalm 109:1-2 & 13 adds: *"Hold not thy peace, O God of my praise; for the mouth of the wicked and the mouth of the deceitful are opened against me: they have spoken against me with a lying tongue... Let his posterity be cut off; and in the generation following let their name be blotted out."*

The name of a disobedient person shall fade away. That is, it shall not last over time. There are many homes that have faded away, many families whose line has ended, and many marriages that have collapsed due to the curse of disobedience. Obedience will keep your home together because the blessings of God shall rest upon the home of an obedient person.

In *Genesis 7:1* Noah and all his family members were saved by God because of Noah's obedience to God. There are blessings that have been ordained for the home of an obedient person.

Psalm 37:25 says: *"I have been young, and now am old; yet have I not seen the righteous forsaken, nor his seed begging bread."* This teaches that God will supply the needs of the children of an obedient person. There will always be provisions for them. The good work of their parents will speak for them in their difficult times.

Psalm 102:28 promises the blessing of descendants to those who obey: *"The children of thy servants shall continue, and their seed shall be established before thee."*

Proverbs 11:21 says that obedience and goodness will win in the end, because God is a God of justice: *"Though hand join in hand, the wicked shall not be unpunished: but the seed of the righteous shall be delivered."* Obedience to God can bring deliverance to your home when dangers come.

In *Luke 1:5-7*, the marriage of Zecharias and Elizabeth endured barrenness, despite the fact that *"they were both righteous before God, walking in all the commandments and ordinances of the Lord blameless."* God kept their home together through all the attacks the marriage suffered because Elizabeth was unable to have children. The barrenness that has broken many homes could not split the home of this couple because they loved and obeyed God. And in the end, God gave them victory over barrenness.

Obedience to God is recognition by your home that God is supreme. It shows that you honour God, and wherever God receives honour, He stays in that place. When God dwells in your home, it will be unbreakable. No challenge can break such a home. The home will always triumph over all its hardships because God is present and at work. Obey God, and encourage members of your family to obey Him too.

3. WISDOM

Wisdom is the application of knowledge to your own advantage. A wise man will apply knowledge to bring positive improvement to his life. There are two types of wisdom: worldly and heavenly wisdom. The ability of your home to stay together will be determined by the kind of wisdom you apply in all issues that concern your family.

James 3:13-18 says: *"Who is a wise man and endued with knowledge among you? Let him shew out of a good conversation his works with meekness of wisdom. But if ye have bitter envying and strife in your hearts, glory not, and lie not against the truth. This wisdom descendeth not from above, but is earthly, sensual, devilish. For where envying and strife is, there is confusion and every evil work. But the wisdom that is from above is first pure, then peaceable, gentle, and easy to be intreated, full of mercy and good fruits, without partiality, and without hypocrisy. And the fruit of righteousness is sown in peace of them that make peace."*

From this passage of Scripture, the two types of wisdom can be compared by the qualities listed:

Purity: Wisdom from heaven has no evil or contamination. It is full of righteousness. If your solution to your family matters does not show righteousness, it is not of God. Any idea that glorifies and embraces sin will attract negative consequences.

Peace: Wisdom from heaven promotes peace, while that of the world is full of strife. You will keep your home together if you promote peace in all situations. If you can embrace peace and live with your spouse in peace, it will become difficult for the enemy to destroy your home.

Gentleness: Wisdom from heaven is gentle and able to tolerate. You will be able to keep your home together if you are gentle in both words and action. Gentleness will enable you to avoid breaking the heart of your spouse. A gentle person is soft-hearted.

Openness to change: Wisdom from above makes you flexible and "easy to be intreated". It makes you amenable to persuasion. Your spouse, when he or she is right about something, will be able to convince you to change your decisions for the benefit of your home. Wisdom from this world does not change position because its selfish nature is arrogant.

Mercy: A merciful person is forgiving and kind. Wisdom from heaven treats people with understanding. It always gives people another chance when they blow the first chance. Always be ready to overlook offence and move on with life, instead of bearing grudges or dwelling on an issue for too long. Wisdom from this world does not show mercy, neither does it help the weak to get stronger.

Good fruits: Heavenly wisdom is full of good fruits – it results in good, not evil. If you apply heavenly wisdom into your family situation, you will always do well for your spouse. Wisdom from this world is full of evil.

Impartiality: Wisdom from heaven is not a respecter of persons. It gives equal treatment to people. Don't exalt your parents and relatives above your spouse. Correct in love and avoid inequality in your home.

Without hypocrisy: Wisdom from heaven is sincere and does not deceive, whereas earthly wisdom suggests that deception can be beneficial. And sometimes, it can be – temporarily – but there will be a bigger price to pay at the end, when lies and deceit are exposed. Sincerity will keep your home from danger. Always tell the truth in all situations. Don't say one thing and then do another. Keep your integrity.

A CASE STUDY OF HEAVENLY WISDOM

"And when Abigail saw David, she hasted, and lighted off the ass, and fell before David on her face, and bowed herself to the ground, and fell at his feet, and said, Upon

me, my lord, upon me let this iniquity be: and let thine handmaid, I pray thee, speak in thine audience, and hear the words of thine handmaid. Let not my lord, I pray thee, regard this man of Belial, even Nabal: for as his name is, so is he; Nabal is his name, and folly is with him: but I thine handmaid saw not the young men of my lord, whom thou didst send.

Now therefore, my lord, as the LORD liveth, and as thy soul liveth, seeing the LORD hath withholden thee from coming to shed blood, and from avenging thyself with thine own hand, now let thine enemies, and they that seek evil to my lord, be as Nabal. And now this blessing which thine handmaid hath brought unto my lord, let it even be given unto the young men that follow my lord. I pray thee, forgive the trespass of thine handmaid: for the LORD will certainly make my lord a sure house; because my lord fighteth the battles of the LORD, and evil hath not been found in thee all thy days.

Yet a man is risen to pursue thee, and to seek thy soul: but the soul of my lord shall be bound in the bundle of life with the LORD thy God; and the souls of thine enemies, them shall he sling out, as out of the middle of a sling. And it shall come to pass, when the LORD shall have done to my lord according to all the good that he hath spoken concerning thee, and shall have appointed thee ruler over Israel; that this shall be no grief unto thee, nor offence of heart unto my lord, either that thou hast shed blood causeless, or that my lord hath avenged himself: but

THE STRAWS OF MARRIAGE

when the LORD shall have dealt well with my lord, then remember thine handmaid.

And David said to Abigail, Blessed be the LORD God of Israel, which sent thee this day to meet me: and blessed be thy advice, and blessed be thou, which hast kept me this day from coming to shed blood, and from avenging myself with mine own hand. For in very deed, as the LORD God of Israel liveth, which hath kept me back from hurting thee, except thou hadst hasted and come to meet me, surely there had not been left unto Nabal by the morning light any that pisseth against the wall.

So David received of her hand that which she had brought him, and said unto her, Go up in peace to thine house; see, I have hearkened to thy voice, and have accepted thy person." **1 Samuel 25:23-35**

Abigail demonstrated heavenly wisdom to quench the evil that was about to befall her family. Lessons from the above story include:

1. She took a stand against her husband's evil. Abigail showed kindness to the people her husband treated badly. If you refuse to join in your spouse's sinful actions, you will save your home from many disasters.

2. She pleaded for her husband. Despite the fact that she did not like what her husband had done, she still pleaded for him. She knew that whatever affected her husband would directly affect her. A wise person will

always seek the good of his or her spouse, even when the spouse does not recognise the need for it.

3. She openly condemned evil. This softened the mind of an angry David who had come to attack her family. If you condemn the evil your spouse does to an outsider, you will soften the heart of the person and avert evil. Abigail condemned her husband's action, dissociating herself from that action, but pleaded for mercy. This softened the mind of David. Her wisdom opened the door for the Spirit of God to intervene in the matter. Let the world know that you don't condone evil in your home, and this will encourage mercy towards members of your family that do wrong. Don't support your spouse against outsiders when it is clear that your spouse is in the wrong, then you will be able to project a good image of your home to outsiders.

4. She talked with understanding. Abigail helped David to understand the repercussions of revenge on his destiny. She talked with wisdom that David could not deny. She was able to win David over. With wisdom, you can win the enemy of your home over and save your home from danger.

5. Abigail's advice averted revenge and promoted peace and forgiveness. Let your counsel promote peace and forgiveness and you will protect your home from the destruction unforgiveness brings.

6. Through wisdom, Abigail was able to avert the evil that was decreed against her family. Even if your spouse brings evil home, with wisdom, you can avert it and save your home from calamity.

4. FAITH

"Now faith is the substance of things hoped for, the evidence of things not seen." **Hebrews 11:1**

To keep your home together, you will need faith in the power of God.

There are many things you may hope for concerning your home. You may hope for positive changes in certain areas of your marriage. You may want your spouse to lose some bad habits and start some good ones. You may be trusting God for your finances to improve. You may desire that your children change for the better. You might be praying for sick members of your family to get well, or you may be believing for a better job for your spouse.

You are hoping for changes you don't see, but you know they are possible. Some changes can only be brought about by the God who established marriage. Faith will help you to wait for God. You must have faith that situations in your marriage will change for the better. You must have faith that your 'bad' spouse can become good tomorrow. You must trust God that a house that is filled with strife and confusion today can become very peaceful tomorrow. You must commit everything into the hand of God, who alone has the ability to grant any change you desire, irrespective of how hard it appears.

Faith will help you to avoid irrational decisions that would bring down your marriage. There is no one God can't change. It was God who changed Paul in *Acts 9*. The same person who had persecuted the people of God started promoting the very faith that he had tried to destroy. Change is possible. There is no situation that God can't change.

It was God who turned childless Hannah into fruitful Hannah in 1 Samuel 1. It was God who restored to Job, more than he had lost, in Job 42. Change is possible. A poor person of today can become a lender tomorrow. You must have faith and refuse the negative suggestion that the present situation is impossible to change. With faith in God, you will be able to keep your marriage together by trusting Him to bring the changes you desire. If your home is facing any challenge, join forces with your spouse to fight it. Don't lose hope for change, because with God nothing is impossible.

5. PRAYER

Prayer is a straw that can hold your marriage together. Marriage is a spiritual institution because the two human beings involved in it are joined more in spirit than in flesh. Therefore, most of the issues in marriage have their roots in the spirit and can only be dealt with spiritually. Prayer opens a way to handle spiritual matters spiritually. Prayer binds things together. A couple who pray together will stay together. Choose the path of prayer to handle all things in your marriage. Before putting any suggestions into action, pray first.

"Then David returned to bless his household…"
2 Samuel 6:20

David went home to bless his home. Learn how to invoke blessings upon your home. Avoid cursing. When you are on your knees, you can transform your spouse from bad to good and you can change the hearts of your children. You can't make any human being better through force. Only prayer can touch areas no human being can touch.

"And it was so, when the days of their feasting were gone about, that Job sent and sanctified them, and rose up early in the morning, and offered burnt offerings according to the number of them all: for Job said, It may be that my sons have sinned, and cursed God in their hearts. Thus did Job continually." Job 1:5

Job rose early to make a sacrifice for his family. As a parent, learn how to rise early to commit the way of your home into the hand of God. Prayer holds homes together. Present your concerns about your home to God in prayer. Avoid irrational decisions that exalt human wisdom above that of God. Pray and pray until you see the changes you desire.

Chapter Seven

COMMUNICATION IN MARRIAGE

Communication is the process of transferring a message between a sender and a receiver. The message could be a piece of information, a feeling or an idea. It is impossible for a marriage to succeed without effective communication.

When people involved in a relationship stop communicating, their relationship starts to die. When a couple experience prolonged communication problems, it will not be long before they separate. Communication in marriage is unique and it requires a unique approach for it to be effective.

UNIQUENESS OF COMMUNICATION IN MARRIAGE

> *"Therefore shall a man leave his father and his mother, and shall cleave unto his wife: and they shall be one flesh."* **Genesis 2:24**

Marriage means two people of the opposite sex sharing 'one flesh'. This kind of relationship can only be found in marriage, because 'one flesh' means far more than sexual intercourse – it refers to unity in body, soul and mind. This is what makes communication in marriage unique.

Whenever a spouse is talking to his or her partner, that person is indirectly talking to him or herself. This implies that you need to talk to your spouse the way you want him or her to talk to you. This is what usually happens in marriage. It is only a matter of time before your spouse will be talking to you the way you talk to him or her. If you keep on talking rudely to your spouse, very soon, he or she will start talking rudely to you, knowingly or unknowingly. And very soon, you also will be talking to your spouse in the way that he or she talks to you. You share the same flesh and you will react to situations in a similar manner.

You can't communicate to your spouse the way you communicate to other people. Let us consider some examples of people you communicate with in life:

1. **Your children**

They are under your training and very soon, your children will leave your house for independent living. You can't talk to your spouse the way you talk to your children, because your spouse has come to stay with you throughout your lifetime. Also your spouse is not under your training — he or she is already an adult and should be treated as such.

2. **In-laws**

Your in-laws don't have covenant relationships with you; only your spouse does. You can't talk to your spouse the way you talk to your in-laws. You see your in-laws occasionally, but you see your spouse all the time. Your spouse is different from your in-laws and you must give him or her that regard.

3. Parents

As an adult, you have to separate from your parents to begin independent living. Your parents are supposed to have limited control and access into your life as an adult, but this is not applicable to your spouse. Your spouse should have full access. You can't communicate to your spouse the way you do with your parents. While your parents know a lot about you, your spouse does not, especially in the early days of marriage, and he or she needs more openness from you for better intimacy. Your spouse deserves a closer relationship and communication than your parents.

4. Boss at work

The relationship between you and your boss at work is official and it is controlled by the terms of your employment. You can't talk to your spouse the way you do with your manager or employer. You can't be official and formal with your spouse as you do at work. You must recognise the limitation of boundaries in certain relationships. You should not expect your spouse to be official and formal when addressing you at home. There is no boundary in marriage.

5. Friends

They come and go but your marriage remains. It is unwise to exalt your friends above your spouse. You can be careless when talking to your friends but you can't do the same with your spouse. At times, due to closeness, people lose respect for each other as friends, but this is not acceptable in marriage. You must recognise the boundary.

6. God

He knows the thoughts of your heart but your spouse can't. You can communicate to God through your heart without uttering words, but you can't do the same with your spouse. You should not expect your spouse to know your mind in every situation. Your spouse will only know for certain what you say, not what you are thinking in your mind. Some people will blame their spouses for not knowing their feelings about certain things. But this is unfair. Unless you express your feelings in words, it is difficult for your spouse to know your feelings in all situations.

METHODS OF COMMUNICATION

There are different methods of communication that exist in human relationships. As time passes and certain events unfold in marriage, couples fall into different ways of communication – whether they are aware of it or not.

There are two methods of communication in human relationships and these are:

1. Verbal communication

This is communication by talking. Words are expressed to pass a message across to each other, and have the power to influence the receiver. There are different kinds of words that people use – good and bad. A home that will stand must embrace good words. Let's look at examples of both.

Bad words

How do you know that your word is bad? Your word is bad if it falls into any of the following groups.

a. **A grievous word.** This is a kind of word that breeds anger. It causes annoyance in the receiver. Your spouse does not want to hear such a word because it causes severe irritation in his or her heart. *Proverbs 15:1* says: *"A soft answer turneth away wrath: but grievous words stir up anger."* Don't distress your spouse with criticism. It brings pain into the heart of the receiver. If your words make your spouse weep, it could be because you utter words that give him or her pains of the heart.

b. **A disrespectful word.** This is a word that is filled with insult and lack of regard. *Malachi 3:13* says: *"Your words have been stout against me, saith the LORD. Yet ye say, What have we spoken so much against thee?"* You must observe respect when communicating to your spouse. If your speech makes your spouse feel small and insulted, it means you are disrespectful in word. Arrogant words belittle the receiver and they spoil good communication.

c. **A flattering word.** *Psalm 12:2* says: *"They speak vanity every one with his neighbour: with flattering lips and with a double heart do they speak."* On the face of it, flattery seems nice, but flattery is actually deception because it isn't sincere. Such deceptive praise is not praise at all. An insincere compliment is flattery. If you can't say something sincerely, find something you can genuinely praise in a person. The speaker of flattering words operates "with a double heart". The truth is kept in the heart while the deception is spoken out. When your spouse discovers that you have been flattering him or her and that you were not genuine, he or she will not believe your words again, and this hinders good communication.

d. **A malicious word.** This kind of word is clearly spiteful and harmful to the receiver. It causes discomfort or hurt. *3 John 1:10* says: *"Wherefore, if I come, I will remember his deeds which he doeth, prating against us with malicious words: and not content therewith, neither doth he himself receive the brethren, and forbiddeth them that would, and casteth them out of the church."* Spiteful, nasty, cruel words harm the feelings of your spouse.

e. **An insincere word.** This is a word that generates false impressions in the receiver towards the speaker. It is a word spoken by a pretender, who is faking godliness. He pretends to be kind but soon his or her actions will show he is far from it. *2 Peter 2:3* says: *"And through covetousness shall they with feigned words make merchandise of you: whose judgment now of a long time lingereth not, and their damnation slumbereth not."* Insincere people are crafty and their words are fake. You will lose the respect of your spouse if it becomes clear that you have not been sincere in your word. This brings mistrust into communication.

f. **A hasty word.** A word spoken in a hurry can be thoughtless and mistaken, which can cause untold damage in a relationship. Think before you speak, because hasty words can be irrational and lead the receiver down the wrong path. A rash decision is usually one you will regret. *Proverbs 29:20* says: *"Seest thou a man that is hasty in his words? there is more hope of* *a fool than of him."* Words spoken in a hurry introduce misconceptions and erroneous conclusions, because they haven't been thought through. And of course, if you speak too fast, it's likely that the hearer will miss part of what you're saying or misunderstand it. If your spouse always complains that he or she does not understand clearly what you are saying, slow down and explain what you want to say more carefully. You don't want your spouse to get a twisted or inaccurate message.

g. **A vain word.** A vain word may not be about vanity; this old English word means "futile" or "useless". Such a word has no bearing on the topic under discussion. It achieves nothing. In *Job 16:3*, Job asks: *"Shall vain words have an end? or what emboldeneth thee that thou answerest?"* A vain word is an empty, pointless word. If you always speak vain words, your spouse will soon lose interest in discussing vital issues with you because your word does not address the topic under discussion. Soon your spouse will no longer take your words seriously.

Bad words destroy communication because they make spouses avoid engaging each other in conversation. Rather, they will prefer to share their secrets with outsiders. Bad words constantly generate friction in communication and build a wall between spouses. Mind your words when you talk to your spouse.

Good words

You are a speaker of a good word if it falls into any of these following groups.

a. **A right word.** This is a word spoken at the right time – a timely word. It addresses the issue at hand. It is a word a person needs for his or her present situation. *Proverbs 15:23* says *"… a word spoken in due season, how good is it!"* Timing is important in communication. For example, you don't argue with your spouse when he or she is in a bad mood. Your spouse wants to hear words that address his or her present fear, worry or concern. Right words spoken at a wrong time will not be appreciated – and so become the wrong words. Use wisdom in communication. Know the right time for certain words.

b. **A comforting word.** Comforting words soothe a sorrowful heart. They drive away fear and anxiety. When your spouse is upset, he or she needs a word that will calm him or her down. Isaiah wrote: *"The Lord GOD hath given me the tongue of the learned, that I should know how to speak a word in season to him that is weary"* (50:4). A person feeling hopeless needs a word that gives hope; someone feeling hurt needs a word of comfort. The kind of word a weak person wants to hear is the word that can strengthen the heart, not a word that adds sorrow to sorrow. When your spouse is tired and weak, don't engage him or her in a long conversation full of arguments and questioning. It will lead to provocation. Many problems of communication in marriage are due to lack of consideration of the other person's feelings.

c. **A kind word.** This is a soft word. Such a word gives strength to the receiver. It takes away fear and gives assurance. In *Genesis 50:21* Joseph eased his brothers' worries by saying: *"Now therefore fear ye not: I will nourish you, and your little ones. And he comforted them, and spake kindly unto them."* Your spouse needs kind words during his or her time of stress and anxiety. Let your words be soft, caring, considerate and compassionate. Unkind words will make your spouse feel threatened.

d. **A gracious word.** Grace is compassion in action. Only the merciful person has a gracious word. Jesus' words were gracious: *"And all bare him witness, and wondered at the gracious words which proceeded out of his mouth. And they said, Is not this Joseph's son?"* (Luke 4:22). Such words give pleasure and satisfaction to the receiver. It is a word that makes people rejoice. If your spouse enjoys speaking with you, it could be that your word is full of grace and it makes your spouse happy whenever you speak. If this is your testimony, keep it up!

e. **A pleasant word.** *Proverbs 16:24* says: *"Pleasant words are as an honeycomb, sweet to the soul, and health to the bones."* A pleasant word sounds very sweet to hear. It gives healing to the receiver. This is a word that brings life to a dead situation. It gives motivation and drives away darkness. Your spouse wants to hear such words, especially when he or she is facing discouragement and uncertainty. May God make you a speaker of pleasant words in Jesus' name.

f. **A wise word.** This is a word that brings a solution to a problem. A wise word makes a way where there seems to be no way. When it is spoken, the receiver taps knowledge from it. *Proverbs 12:18* says a wise word is a healing word: *"There is that speaketh like the piercings of a sword: but the tongue of the wise is health."* Wisdom heals and takes away the wounds of many years. The speaker of a wise word will save his or her spouse from evil.

The kind of word you speak to your spouse will determine the effectiveness of communication in your marriage. If your words are bad, you will soon create a communication barrier between yourself and your spouse. If your words are good, you will be able to strengthen your relationship with your spouse through effective communication.

> *"The lips of the righteous know what is acceptable: but the mouth of the wicked speaketh frowardness."*
> **Proverbs 10:32**

This proverb shows that who you are will influence how you talk. Your words will be good if you love God and live a holy life. If God dwells inside of you, whenever you open your mouth to speak, you can use the words of the Spirit of God, not yourself. Unfortunately, even as Christians, we have a sinful nature that must be 'crucified' – put to death on a daily basis – and we must continually ask God to fill us with His Spirit. If we are doing this, we can speak the words of the Spirit – the words of life.

If you have communication problems in your marriage, check your relationship with God.

2. Non-verbal communication

This is communication by signs instead of words. There is a type of body language which operates in all conversations, but here we are talking about something more extreme than that. Some couples have such serious verbal communication problems that their interaction descends into non-verbal means of communication. They express their feelings and opinions in this way rather than talking, because they are fed up of arguments, or are afraid of starting an argument.

Examples of non-verbal means of communication found in many homes include:

1. Silence

When there is an issue, instead of the couple sitting down to have a serious talk, they end up keeping silent. This may be due to fear on the part of one spouse, or it may be malicious – a refusal to talk, as a form of punishment of the other spouse.

At times, one partner will refuse to talk to the other as a way of expressing displeasure concerning certain issues. It has become a tradition in some homes that whenever one of the spouses keeps quiet in an unusual manner, it is a sign of lack of satisfaction about a particular problem in the marriage. Refusing to speak to your spouse is actually a form of emotional abuse, as it deprives your spouse of a natural means of expression. Fear of talking is a different issue, as it is usually a feature of the victim of emotional or even physical abuse, rather than the perpetrator.

In *2 Samuel 13:22*, Absalom refused to talk to his brother because he was angry with him for raping his sister, and after two years, he killed his brother. Malice and silence is a breeding ground for the devil to sow seeds of unforgiveness and bitterness. It creates room for suspicion and wrong conclusions. It complicates matters in the home. The home will be filled with uncertainty. Never use malicious silence as a way of expressing your feelings to your spouse. Break the silence and talk over all concerns prayerfully, and then you will defeat the devil's scheme.

2. Crying

Weeping occurs when emotions become uncontrollable, and it is a natural expression of feelings about certain situations in the marriage. In some homes, when one of the spouses begins to cry, the other partner immediately knows that he or she is not happy about a certain issue that affects their marriage. If you don't know why your spouse is crying, then it is your responsibility to find out why and to try to resolve the problem.

In *1 Samuel 1:8*, Elkanah knew that Hannah's crying was an expression of her sorrow concerning her barrenness. Crying relieves the emotional pressure building up inside a person. However, although it may bring some internal relief to the spouse concerned, it also creates confusion in the other partner. Men in particular often don't know how to handle a situation where their spouse is weeping. Crying can cause issues to be handled emotionally rather than intelligently. It can even be used by some spouses to emotionally manipulate their partner, creating sympathy in order to get their own way on a particular issue. Such pretence is bad for a marriage, and if realised by the other partner, will result in a lack of sympathy when the spouse is genuinely upset or hurting.

When emotions are allowed too much sway, the heart begins to rule the head, resulting in errors in decisions.

COMMUNICATION IN MARRIAGE

Weeping without words can also result in the other partner misreading the feeling and the information the weeping partner is trying to get across. Many a time, in order to prevent the other partner from crying further, wrong solutions may be applied to please him or her. This could have detrimental effects upon the home in future. It is better to talk than to cry, though genuine tears are a perfectly natural overflow of emotion and should be a warning to the other spouse of the depth of emotion involved.

3. Beating

This is used in some homes to communicate displeasure over certain issues in the marriage. Some men use beating to let their spouse know that they are not happy with their spouse's behaviour, words or efforts. Some men believe that unless they beat their wife, their complaints will not be taken seriously. But using violence to communicate is of the devil, not God, and is never justified.

Proverbs 10:12 says: *"Hatred stirreth up strifes: but love covereth all sins."* Beating is an expression of hatred, not a means of communication. Violence endangers the health and life of your partner, and anything could happen during or after beating. You are following the devil if you beat your spouse. Your prayers to God will never receive an answer because you can't use the same hands that beat your spouse to take your requests to God in prayer. God will not listen to you whilst you behave in this way.

You must be able to talk over a matter without resorting to physical abuse. If you are frustrated by your spouse or don't think that he or she listens to you or takes your complaints seriously, it is still no excuse to slap, punch, kick, etc. You should never even threaten violence, never mind carry it out. Rather, if you are unable to resolve issues by discussion with your partner, you should ask a counsellor to help you to come to agreement. And of course, you should take the problem to the Lord in prayer, asking Him to help you find a peaceful solution.

4. **Facial expression**

This is the use of your face to express your feelings. It could be as simple as a glance in your direction when you mention a certain subject. When there is an issue at home, one of the partners flashes his or her face at the other partner and the other partner knows what it means, because he or she has been experiencing it for a long time in the relationship.

It can sometimes be a 'knowing glance' that merely expresses agreement, or a smile expressed towards you which is a sign of approval. But faces can also express displeasure – a menacing glance or a furious face can speak volumes without saying a word. But provided your conversation is not in public, it is much better to air your grievances or disagreement using words instead of facial expressions. For a start, they can be misinterpreted – it is often difficult to judge an expression correctly – whereas you can make yourself clear with words. Facial expressions can also be ignored, so it is always better to talk things through.

5. **Shouting**

I'm classing shouting as non-verbal because the same words spoken gently can have a very different impact and meaning to words shouted.

Some people shout or even 'bark' to express their feelings about situations. This is very common with an aggressive spouse. Shouting is used to express displeasure about a matter. Shouting erodes the beauty of a good relationship, and is a sign of wanting to seize control or override the opinion of the other person. It is the opposite of good communication. If you try to dominate a conversation by shouting you will only cause either fear or greater antagonism in your spouse. Both are damaging to a relationship.

Shouting can cause panic, create confusion and disrupt concentration. It also turns a discussion into an argument – exacerbating the problem. An immature spouse uses shouting as a method of communication. It can also be a sign of insecurity, indicating that you are not sure that your opinion will be given proper consideration if you don't ram it home with volume. Avoid raising your voice when talking to your spouse. Let your spouse feel safe in talking to you. Just talk and make yourself clear. Shouting is a sign of disrespect; avoid it in your marriage.

6. Letter writing

Communication has gone so bad in some homes that the partners resort to letter writing. Often it is a final resort – when couples are on the brink of separation. Of course, you can also write a love letter, which is a beautiful thing, and sometimes letters can be used to cool a heated debate. But often letter-writing is a result of insecurity. One partner who feels intimidated in communication may resort to letter writing to his or her partner as a way of escaping the intimidation.

If your spouse likes writing letters to you to express his or her opinion concerning certain family issues, it is an indication that he or she feels insecure when talking to you. You need to examine yourself. If this is prolonged, it will result in disunity and the purpose of living together as husband and wife will be eroded. There will be no sharing of the hearts.

Another problem with letter writing, or emails or texting, is that such written words can be more easily misunderstood than if expressed verbally. When you talk face to face with someone, your expressions, inflections, tone and body language can all ensure that your communication is correctly understood. These personal expressions cannot be seen in letters, texts and emails. If you are temporarily in separate locations for work or other reasons, try Skype or other systems where you can see the person's face on a computer screen, mobile phone or other digital device. At least then, you can see them as they talk and gain a better impression of the feelings behind the words.

HUMAN NATURE IN COMMUNICATION

There are clear differences between a man and a woman, and when they marry they must learn how to recognise and manage those differences. Irrespective of the level of spirituality of a man or a woman, their human nature reflects in the way that they talk. Men are wired to function in a different way to women. This was done by God to enable an individual to function according to the purpose of God.

1 Peter 3:7 says: *"Likewise, ye husbands, dwell with them according to knowledge, giving honour unto the wife, as unto the weaker vessel, and as being heirs together of the grace of life; that your prayers be not hindered."* Here Peter is advising husbands to deal with their wives with understanding – in other words: be considerate.

This cuts both ways – we need to be considerate of each other's differences. The sexes are very different from each other, and the gender of an individual contributes to the way he or she communicates. This understanding must be brought into your communication as a married couple. With understanding, you will not personalise every word you hear from your spouse, but you will see it as a manifestation of human nature. As a man or a woman surrenders certain areas of his or her life to the authority of the Holy-Spirit, the fallen nature starts disappearing gradually and the person becomes another person. We begin to think and talk differently, as our hearts begin to be more in tune with the Spirit.

But in the meantime, while this process is going on, we need to appreciate the inherent nature of a man and a woman. It takes time to be transformed by the Holy Spirit.

Let us look at how a man and a woman were designed to function and how this affects the way they talk, until the Holy Spirit changes all areas of our lives – including communication.

1. The natural man

> *"And the LORD God took the man, and put him into the garden of Eden to dress it and to keep it."* **Genesis 2:15**

> *"And unto Adam he said, Because thou hast hearkened unto the voice of thy wife, and hast eaten of the tree, of which I commanded thee, saying, Thou shalt not eat of it: cursed is the ground for thy sake; in sorrow shalt thou eat of it all the days of thy life; thorns also and thistles shall it bring forth to thee; and thou shalt eat the herb of the field; in the sweat of thy face shalt thou eat bread, till thou return unto the ground; for out of it wast thou taken: for dust thou art, and unto dust shalt thou return."*
> ***Genesis 3:17-19***

Man was created to be the head of the family, and he was able to easily provide for his wife in the Garden of Eden, where everything good to eat grew in abundance. But after the fall of man in the Garden, he was sent out to start fending for himself and his family members. This has modified his nature and the way he functions as a provider.

For example, man has a hunting nature which he developed through searching for provisions for his family. He pursues food to bring it home for his family. He is always thinking of how to take care of his home. It is his responsibility to care for the home, and in times past he had to fight animals to bring something home for his family. Of course, there would also be plant food to be gathered, but being physically stronger the man was more capable than the woman of killing animals for meat. This has made man more naturally aggressive than woman, because he needs to be aggressive to feed his family. In a fallen world, man also had to defend his family – against predatory animals

COMMUNICATION IN MARRIAGE

or other men. He literally had to fight for the survival of his family.

The problem with this aggressive nature is that if it is not well managed, it can reflect in the way he talks to his wife. Some men are very aggressive in their speech and language. This destroys good communication in the marriage. If you are an aggressive man, you need to invite the Holy Spirit to help you to be gentle. You should be aggressive in the spirit, not in the physical realm, unless your family is threatened.

Furthermore, man tends to be more single-focussed. Focus is an attribute needed for a hunter to be able to catch his prey. It helps a man to do one thing at a time. This attribute is good because it will help you as a man not to miss the blessings God sends to you for the benefit of your family. Nevertheless, the wife needs to understand that due to the more focussed nature of man, he is less likely to be able to concentrate on many topics than a woman. Men can become irritated and confused. Therefore, in communication, it is better if the wife deals with one issue at once.

As a woman, don't feel offended when your husband remains quiet for a long time during communication. It could be that you are bringing in so many topics into one discussion that he is having to think them all through. Don't feel insulted that he is not replying to all of your conversation, that is his nature. But after some time, as both of you surrender to the work of the Holy Spirit on your personalities, you will understand the best approach to use when communicating with each other.

As a woman, you will also soon discover that men like to offer solutions to every problem, even when you did not ask for a solution! If you raise a question, expect your husband to want to find an answer. A person that is the head of a family must have enough intelligence to navigate his family out of problems. An average man must be a carrier of solutions. That is his nature and it is an essential requirement to be the head of a home.

Therefore, don't be offended as a woman if you notice that whenever you are talking to your husband, he likes offering solutions instead of listening to you. This means he might interrupt your flow, as he may want to share a solution that has occurred to him – before he forgets it!

Some women have complained that their husbands present themselves as if they know everything, and this makes women feel angry. Often it's true that men are too egotistical, wanting to show off how good they are, and so it's natural for women to react against this. Many women have entered into serious arguments with their husband in an attempt to convince the man that he does not know everything. But beware, if you undermine your husband's self-confidence in this way, you may undermine his feeling of self-worth. And a man who feels inferior to his wife is unlikely to be a happy husband, which will have consequences for the marital relationship.

Rightly, though, women feel insulted if their husbands don't listen to their own opinions in matters that affect their families. Husbands have a natural inclination to want their views to be the ones that win out. It is the human nature of man to behave as a problem solver, and if he's not solving the problems then he feels useless or even that his life is pointless. It takes time for a man to develop a confidence that does not rely on his own abilities but on God's. It is the work of the Holy Spirit.

Therefore, as a woman, don't personalise it when you notice this nature in your husband. His desire to be right about everything does not mean he loves you any less, and it is not intended to belittle you. But it is an indication that more prayer is needed in the family to break the man's pride down so that he can listen to his wife's view and value her opinion. Men who have been married longer tend to appreciate their wife's opinion more than they did when they were younger, as a result of experience! So many men have lost a lot of wonderful ideas God sent to them through their wives because of their pride and egotistical nature.

It is also important to note that a man prefers a brief story or comment, rather than a long-winded description of a problem. That's because he enjoys solving the problem and wants to get onto that as soon as possible! So, as a woman, you should not feel insulted when you notice that your husband is too brief in his comment about your long story, or interrupts you to start offering solutions. It is not because he has something against you, but because of his human nature – and because of his desire to help you.

2. The natural woman

> *"Unto the woman he said, I will greatly multiply thy sorrow and thy conception; in sorrow thou shalt bring forth children; and thy desire shall be to thy husband, and he shall rule over thee."* **Genesis 3:16**

This verse indicates that women were not only given a body capable of bearing children, but are wired to rear children. They are designed to care for their children. They have a special bond with their children, and this reflects in their reaction to issues that affect their children.

As a man you may notice that your wife is over-protective and sometimes unrealistic whenever you are discussing issues affecting your children. You should not take this personally. It is a result of the bond between her and the child. Generally speaking, women don't take issues affecting their children lightly. It is an inherent nature in them. They love their children in a special way.

This may have its origin in the fact that women carry their children alone for a good nine months before delivery. In that time, they were physically and emotionally connected to their children. They remember the pain they went through whenever they see their children. This makes them react sentimentally towards issues surrounding their children. As a man you should show understanding when your wife seems to worry too much about issues that concern your children.

Furthermore, for a woman to be able to perform the role of child bearing, certain chemicals must be present in her body to cause all the unique but necessary changes in the body. Women have certain chemicals and hormones that enable them to be pregnant, carry babies for nine months, and breastfeed. All these chemicals and reactions cause variation in the moods of women, and this may reflect in the way they talk, particularly at the time of the month of their period. Your wife may become unnecessarily aggressive in conversations during this time. Alternatively, you may notice a reluctance to engage in conversation. The changes in mood and emotions are a reflection of certain chemicals being secreted in her body.

As a man, you must not take everything personally or overreact when you notice certain negativity in the way your wife speaks to you, but rather show more maturity and understanding. Your wife is different from you. God made her different, otherwise she would not be able to perform her role as a child bearer and procreation would have been impossible.

Furthermore, as a man you must also know that women's nurturing nature is likely to extend beyond her own children. It makes her more caring and compassionate about other people. They take care of their children and their husband, but they are also more likely than men to want to care for grandparents, friends and colleagues. In fact, women have a special ability to love because a certain kind of self-sacrificial love is needed to raise children. When women have children they have to put their children first if they are to survive and grow.

Women know how to love and it reflects in their conversation. Women are emotional because love is about showing emotion. Love is a powerful emotion! As a man, you have to learn how to cope and manage the emotions of your wife. Due to her emotional nature, she sometimes cries when she is under stress. That is why you should not subject your wife to too much stress, otherwise you will make her break down emotionally. You must learn how to talk to your wife softly, gently and tenderly.

Also, women enjoy talking because talking promotes love. Women love men that talk. If you are too quiet, your wife may complain and you should show understanding towards her. Women were made to care for people and therefore have a people-focused nature. They focus on relationships, so they love talking about people. Caring is about relationships. This concern about other people can be twisted by temptation into gossip, so women need to be careful about their focus on others. But as a man, don't be surprised when your wife always talks about people. It is the nature of a woman to be people focused. Show understanding when you wife's conversation is full of what other people are saying or doing.

Women also have a stronger ability than men to do several things at the same time, called multi-tasking. This is the case because caring for people needs the ability to handle many things at the same time. If they have several children, who all have different needs at the same time, a mother needs to be able to cope with all these at once. Men are less good at multi-tasking, and are more single-focussed, so on average men get more stressed in a busy home.

Men should also not be surprised that their wife sometimes nags. Nagging is a form of continual complaints and fault-finding. It's not pleasant but it arises from the fact that women are people-focused, always watching behaviour and remembering their words and actions. Women need to control their nagging tendencies if they want their marriage to survive, but equally men need to understand why nagging occurs and not to overreact to it.

As your spouse yields all areas of his or her life to the Holy Spirit, the influence of these natures will disappear. Nevertheless, if you can learn how to laugh over many things in your marriage instead of taking it personally, you will have so much fun at home. When your spouse shows his or her natural self that defines him as a man or her as a woman, turn it around into jokes and in appreciation of the differences between the two of you.

Imagine if both of you were the same in all respects; the relationship would be too boring and monotonous. There is plenty of fun in diversity. God created man and woman to differ in many areas in order to make their lives together eventful. There is no better person in a marriage. It only depends on who manifests his or her weaknesses first. The first to show weaknesses might be considered inferior, but that false impression only lasts until the other person manifests his or her own weaknesses – usually in a bigger form! Let your communication be filled with grace and appreciation of the diversity that exists between the two of you.

BARRIERS TO COMMUNICATION IN MARRIAGE

There are many factors that are responsible for serious barriers in communication between couples. These include:

1. Background

The way a person was brought up in life could affect his or her communication style, especially with the opposite sex. We all come from different homes, culture and social orientation. There are some cultures that prohibit women from looking at a man's face and talking one-on- one. It is considered rude and inappropriate for a woman to talk to her husband looking at his face. A lady brought up under such a culture will feel timid when talking to her husband in marriage. If the man came from a different culture, he may misinterpret his wife's attitude during communication.

Also, some cultures consider women as less intelligent and unequal to men. A man that came from such a culture may not appreciate the opinions of his spouse during communication. The man will appear bossy and domineering in conversation. He will never respect the views of the wife. Such men become dictators at home.

It is also important to note that some people come from homes where they never saw their parents sit down and talk about family matters. When such a person grows up, it will be strange for him or her to be told to sit down and discuss family matters with his or her spouse. If you notice this uncomfortable attitude in your spouse, it will be better for you to seek counselling for both of you, so that your spouse can receive help and be taught about the importance of communication in marriage.

You should appreciate that people come from different homes, and were exposed to different experiences as they grew up in life. It is possible for a person to be unintentionally incommunicative or to have a wrong attitude without knowing it. The problem often lies in the foundation of their lives – their experiences in their early years.

2. Personal beliefs and principles

Personal beliefs and principles can be barriers to communication in marriage. Some of them have their root in the books people have read and the education that people have received. Some people blindly accept the views that certain authors express in their books, and start applying them to their own marriage. Some people have been taught wrong things by blind teachers who have no knowledge about how to make marriage successful.

Some books are written by confused people. This confusion is revealed by the destructive messages they include in their books. Other authors have achieved success in certain areas of their lives but have failed woefully in marriage. Unfortunately, an innocent person may read their books on marriage and unwisely accept all the teaching in the book. The reader believes the message because the author's achievements are impressive, even though the author is no expert in marriage. For example, just because an author is a famous TV star some people naively think that what he says on other subjects must be right. In truth, the only subject the TV star is qualified to write about is his own career. But success in a career doesn't automatically make him knowledgeable about other issues, like marriage. Fame can lend a credibility that really isn't justified.

Even if the author has a successful marriage, that does not mean that everybody should agree with his views on marriage or apply them to their own situation. Every marriage is different, and every person is unique. Some things that may have worked for one marriage will not necessarily work for another. And in any case, the author's success at marriage may be more due to his spouse than himself!

The only thing that is universally true is the Word of God. Personal methods that have no origin in the Word of God may work for certain homes but fail in another. For example, a couple that comes from the same culture or similar upbringing may succeed in using certain methods from their culture which are not found in the Bible. There is a culture and religious belief that considers women as inferior, and if a woman accepts that in her relationship with her husband, they may have success in their marriage because they are fitting in with their culture. But the same principle will cause friction in another home where the spouses have different and opposite religious beliefs or cultural backgrounds. Therefore, you should be careful about books you read on marriage and ideas you receive from so-called experts on the institution of marriage. You must ensure that such ideas agree with the infallible Word of God before you apply them to your marriage.

While it is good to have principles to live by in life, such principles must be in complete agreement with the Bible. Avoid ideas that promote your weaknesses. Reject books that support your wrong attitudes.

3. Past hurts

In Western society, where divorce and family breakdown has become more common over the past few generations, children grow up with emotional damage. These bad experiences then interfere with their own ability to form a stable relationship, and so dysfunctional family life and divorce are now perpetuated from one generation to the next.

Also, what people have experienced in their own adult relationships in the past can affect their views about the opposite sex. Those who have been badly treated in previous relationships will carry anxiety about new relationships. Some have been involved in broken relationships with the opposite sex before they married their present spouses. They bring all the pains and disappointments of the past into the new relationship. They will often have the wrong mindset about the opposite sex. Their views about marriage or the opposite sex will be prejudiced before they enter the marriage. Such individuals relate with suspicion and may misinterpret every word from their spouses. They have a negative attitude about everything concerning their spouses.

Some men will say: "I know how women think." Some women will say: "I know what men are like." The knowledge they are referring to is not of good but evil. Similar expressions might be: "You can't trust men" or "women try to control you". This wrong belief develops in them a wrong attitude to their spouses, even when their spouses are being genuine. Such people never respect the views of their spouses and they show a bad attitude during communication with their spouses. If you always have problem with your spouse during communication, you may need to check your own mind to ensure you have not brought your past hurts and prejudices into your marriage.

4. Attitudes

Some wrong attitudes have a negative effect on communication. You know someone has a bad attitude if they say or do similar wrong things repeatedly. Unless this is dealt with, it will lead to a communication crisis in the marriage. The bad attitude is sponsored by the spirit that is behind it.

Examples of the negative spirits that produce bad attitudes in communication are:

a. **Assertive spirit.** This manifests in the form of aggression and insistence. A partner suffering from this spirit will always insist that his or her opinion should be respected above your own. Aggression will be shown that will frighten the other partner to make him or her to submit to the view being promoted. If this attitude continues in communication, the spouse on the receiving end will start avoiding communication, preferring to be silent rather than discuss issues. When you notice this in your spouse, you may need to check your manner of talking.

   1 Corinthians 9:25 says: "And every man that striveth for the mastery is temperate in all things." Learn how to be temperate in communication. Avoid being aggressive and assertive. Respect the opinion of your spouse.

b. **Argumentative spirit.** This sponsors contentious, combative, belligerent behaviour during communication. The person suffering from this spirit always sees things from a different angle and is fond of turning discussions into arguments. He or she rarely accepts opposite ideas freely. Every opinion from the partner is criticised without close examination. An argumentative person refuses to accept the rational conclusion that results from a discussion.

If you have this attitude, your partner will be very brief when talking to you or, at times, avoid engaging you in any matter that needs deliberation. Your spouse will start operating alone as a way of maintaining peace. When you notice this in your spouse, you will need to talk over it and explore why you always show such a bad attitude. If your spouse is the argumentative one, make it known to your spouse that this is a bad attitude that inhibits your communication.

Proverbs 21:19 says: *"It is better to dwell in the wilderness, than with a contentious and an angry woman"*! The same applies with contentious men. Unreasonable arguing is a reflection of dislike towards what somebody has said. Avoid it. It is dangerous.

c. **Domineering spirit.** This spirit produces imbalance during communication because only one party will do most of the talking. The other person will be a mere observer while the domineering person is busy talking. This spirit operates through the person who considers himself or herself as having better ideas. Such a person does most of the talking in order to promote those ideas.

If this attitude is a continual characteristic of communication, the home will be ruled by the opinions of only one person in the marriage. The interests of the other person will be marginalised, since his or her views are not given any positive consideration. It is only a matter of time before the spouse of the domineering person will lose motivation in discussions, especially in conversations where certain decisions need to be taken. If you notice unusual silence from your partner or reluctant agreement to whatever you say, it could be that you are too domineering in communication and your spouse is trying to avoid talking. Even if you do have better ideas than your partner, you still need to listen to the opinions of your spouse with respect, and to explain why your ideas are better without trying to force those ideas on your partner.

d. **Repetitive spirit.** This spirit manifests through repetition of statements or words. The person suffering from this spirit will keep on saying the same thing over and over again during communication. Some people use it to convey the seriousness of their message, while some use it to hint that they are not prepared to negotiate or compromise on the matter under discussion. For example, in *Judges 16:6-17*, Delilah repeated her request every day until Samson was so fed up that he gave in to her request. Repetition can be used to get your own way, to get your partner to agree to something that you want, but that will often be the wrong decision. And even if you are right, the way you have gone about it will irritate and annoy your partner – as all nagging does.

Whatever the reason for repetition, a repetitive spirit makes communication boring and monotonous. If your partner appears uninterested and sluggish during communication, it could be that you are boring him or her due to your repetition of words.

e. **Spirit of exaggeration.** This spirit operates to mislead the listener in some way, or to draw sympathy. If the aim is sympathy, this spirit makes its victim exaggerate pain or comments or treatment he or she received from somebody. If the aim is to mislead, the person might, for example, make a small thing appear bigger than it really was, or more dangerous, or more exciting, in order to impress the listener.

At times, exaggeration is used when someone wants their spouse to see the seriousness of what he or she is saying. It's a shortcut to getting the result you want, avoiding having to spend a lot of time convincing your spouse of your point. But every deceit has consequences. For example, your exaggeration might cause your spouse to respond in a way you did not anticipate, which may cause trouble. He or she may pass on your exaggeration to others and the lie is spread around. If the news gets to the wrong person – someone who knows what really happened – then your lie will be found out. Exaggeration is just a subtle word for lying.

Proverbs 17:4 says: "A wicked doer giveth heed to false lips; and a liar giveth ear to a naughty tongue." Exaggeration is a lie and it is of the devil. You should stop it in your communication. The more you exaggerate, the more you lie and the more you give the devil a chance to intervene in your marriage matters, because the devil delights in deception.

f. **Lying spirit.** This spirit helps people cover up the truth. Due to fear of being rebuked or humiliated, a spouse may lie during communication so as to cover up the truth. Also, people lie to gain honour from their listeners that isn't due to them, though the day the truth is discovered; they will be less respected than they were in the first place.

You lie to your spouse because you don't want the truth to be known. Sometimes your spouse will act ignorantly based on the lie you have told him or her, and this will later result in disaster. When your spouse discovers that he or she has acted under deceptive words from you, your word will no longer be respected in the family. The next time you engage your spouse in communication, you may notice that your word is not taken seriously, or it is challenged. When you notice this attitude in your spouse you may need to check if you have been lying during communication.

g. **Spirit of criticism.** This spirit sponsors judgement and accusation during communication. A spouse suffering from the critical spirit will fault every word spoken by his or her partner. Your conversation will be laced with criticism. Soon your partner will start feeling uncomfortable and unfairly judged, and will become antagonistic in return. If the situation persists, there will be a communication breakdown at home. If you notice that whenever you talk with your spouse, it always results in accusation and counter-accusation, it means one of you is influenced by the spirit of criticism.

h. **Unyielding spirit.** This spirit makes a person unwilling to change their position on an issue even when it is clear that the opinion of the other person is better than his or her own. A person that suffers from this spirit blindly holds on to his or her own opinions, irrespective of the fact that his or her opinion is unpopular. If you always insist that your opinion is right, and you are not prepared to shift your ground, your spouse may be tempted to resort to individualism. This means that he or she does things in his or her own way, without consulting you. If you notice that your spouse no longer asks you about certain decisions, it could be that you suffer from an unyielding spirit. You need to learn how to be reasonable and surrender to your spouse's view if it is better than yours. It is important to stop being stupidly rigid.

i. **Word-twisting spirit.** This is a spirit that causes wrong interpretation of what is being said. A person that suffers from this spirit will always give the wrong meaning to the word spoken by his or her partner. People like this are easily offended because they interpret the words of their partner as insulting or critical, when in fact their partner has no such intention.

Psalm 56:5 says: "Every day they wrest my words: all their thoughts are against me for evil." In this verse 'wrest' means twist, like a wrestler tries to twist his opponent onto the floor. Spoken words are given a different meaning by the hearer. This can either be a very subtle difference or a completely opposite meaning. Either way it can be harmful. The partner that suffers from this spirit always accuses his or her spouse of hurling insults. If this persists, the spouse may avoid any depth of conversation with the partner due to fear of being misinterpreted or misquoted.

In *2 Peter 3:16* Peter says that the Apostle Paul's words were twisted by people: *"As also in all his epistles, speaking in them of these things; in which are some things hard to be understood, which they that are unlearned and unstable wrest, as they do also the other scriptures, unto their own destruction."*

This indicates that those who suffer from a word-twisting spirit are often people that are unstable or ignorant. They may be emotionally and psychologically unstable. It could also be that they are not good listeners and this makes them miss the true meaning of what they are hearing.

It should be noted that people twist words intentionally and sometimes unintentionally. Some people are trouble makers who knowingly twist the words of their partners and so cause trouble at home. There are also people who twist words unwittingly. They are genuinely ignorant due to their personal weaknesses such as being bad listeners, or they lack education and misunderstand what is being expressed. Word twisters make their victims feel bad because of wrong accusations. If you notice that your spouse always feels bad due to the way you react to his or her words, it could be that you suffer from a word-twisting spirit.

j. **Distractive spirit.** This spirit sponsors the manifestation of past hurt into the present discussion. Bitter words spoken in the past are brought into the present communication. Your partner reminds you of offences or negative comments you have made in the past, in order to undermine whatever point you are making. This complicates what is being discussed in the present. It doesn't help solve the problem; it merely distracts attention from the real problem, which will still need solving later.

Diverting attention to what happened in the past can mean the present discussion is abandoned. This pollutes communication and causes distraction. This habit is very common in the spouse that suffers from unforgiveness and bitterness. Such a person considers the present discussion as an opportunity to express his or her anger about past events in the family. This is the activity of a distractive spirit to shift the focus of the family away from the present matter. If this continues without a change, the family will always dwell on the past and never make progress in life. The couple will always have a lot of unresolved matters in the family.

If you notice that whenever you are discussing issues with your spouse, it always results in distraction, and you end up focussing on what has already happened instead of what is happening and what may happen, it means one of you is suffering from a distractive spirit.

k. **Arrogant spirit.** This spirit sponsors disrespectful words during communication. Communication with an arrogant person will be filled with insults and intimidation. An arrogant spouse ridicules the opinion of his or her partner and exalts his or her own opinion. Arrogant people feel superior to others. They exaggerate the importance of their own opinions. In all discussions, an arrogant spouse wants his or her own view to be accepted in the family.

Similarly, an arrogant person loves to ignore his or her partner during communication, to make the person feel little. An arrogant person pretends not to hear what you are saying because your words are considered less important. He or she appears uninterested in the discussion, which sends a message to the speaker that there is no point in talking. If your words make your spouse feel irritated and angry, it could be that you are suffering from the spirit of arrogance. You are arrogant in communication if your spouse always feels intimidated when talking to you. Soon, your spouse will stop communicating with you. You need to show good manners and a caring approach when talking to your spouse. You must be respectful and polite in communication.

l. **Impatient spirit.** This spirit makes the speaker demand an immediate answer in a matter that needs a longer period of critical thinking. Even if you tell a partner like this of the seriousness of the matter and therefore the importance of wise consideration, the person suffering from an impatient spirit will not listen. He or she pressurises their spouse into giving immediate opinions and answers on a very serious matter. If the partner of an impatient person yields to the pressure and gives a response when ideas have not been well thought through, the home will be heading for disaster due to a wrong decision. If the partner of a person with an impatient spirit refuses to yield to the pressure to give an urgent answer, their action will be wrongly interpreted by the impatient person. This implies that wisdom is needed to calm down an impatient person and make him or her realise the need for detailed consideration before certain decisions are taken in the family.

KNOWING EACH OTHER THROUGH COMMUNICATION

It is possible to use communication to build unity at home. By communicating, you can develop better knowledge of your spouse. If you can engage each other in regular talking and share information together about each other, you will create a home where you and your spouse know each other and this knowledge will help you live together with understanding. People have problems in marriage because they don't know each other very well, often offending each other because they misunderstand each other.

If you talk through the following points with your spouse, you will build up your knowledge of each other:

1. **Weaknesses**

You need to talk together about areas of weakness that each of you have. Examples of weaknesses could be getting angry when tired or not in a good mood; inability to say no to certain demands from people, etc. Be open and honest. Let your spouse know your weaknesses so that he or she can allow for that in your relationship, and respond with more understanding. Bring these weaknesses to the prayer altar to help each other.

2. **Strengths**

Talk through the strengths each of you have. Share areas where you know that you are strong and let your spouse tell you the same. This will help you to know who is best to tackle a certain problem or task. You will be able to treat each other according to the ability of the individual. Knowing the strengths of your spouse will control and guide your expectations from him or her. Examples of strength could be money management, temperance, DIY(do it yourself) skills, etc.

3. **Visions and dreams**

As individuals you had visions and dreams before you got married to each other. These personal visions and dreams need to be harmonised to form a common vision and dream for the family. Share with each other the visions and dreams you have been nurturing for a long time, probably before marriage. From this knowledge, prayerfully combine them to make plans for the whole family. Never pursue an individual vision and dream alone as a married person.

It will become a recipe for individualism in the marriage. Two conflicting or competing visions result in division.

4. Family backgrounds

When you marry a person, you have also married his relatives. You need to share together information about your family backgrounds. Describe to each other your upbringing, your parents' beliefs and personalities, and as much as you know about your family circumstances. This will help your spouse know how to relate with your family members. At times, couples' problems can be traced to their family background. In one family, it may be a tradition to have late child-bearing, while in another family certain sicknesses are common. There is no perfect family. Every family has their own shortcomings. Sharing this kind of information is not to determine whose family is best but to create knowledge about the relatives your spouse will be dealing with. When you notice the manifestation of certain events that are common in your spouse's family, you will be able to deal with it prayerfully. You can engage in prayer warfare against any parental sicknesses or generational evil patterns. If you are more informed about your partner's family you will be more able to pray intelligently for them.

5. Tastes

You need to share with each other your individual tastes. Likes and dislikes must be known in the relationship. Examples of tastes could be the kind of food you love to eat for breakfast, lunch, dinner and supper, the colours you prefer, the kind of shoes and clothes you like most, the type of music you like listening to, how you would like your birthday to be celebrated, etc. The knowledge of tastes will help you know how to satisfy each other's needs, and avoid wasted money on unwanted presents!

6. Friends

It is important to tell each other the kind of friends you have. Explain important things that have happened between you and your friends. What kind of people are they and how is their behaviour? Are they Christians like you? This knowledge will help you and your spouse to decide the level of closeness each of your friends should have in your life. Some friends are only good for you when you are not married, but after marriage, they should separate from you. Some friends are envious and may become jealous of your married happiness, and turn against you or your spouse. So, be wise in who you choose to maintain connections with. Although it is healthy for both of you to continue the best friendships, it is foolish to exalt your friends above your spouse. It is only your spouse that has a covenant relationship with you. When your friends return to their own homes, it is your spouse who will remain with you.

7. The past

Tell each other all about your lives – the good and the bad. Certain events of the past don't die easily, and even after marriage, they can still catch up with you. Don't hide the past from each other. Being open about your past will protect your home against the devil, who likes to use your past to attack your home. Better understanding of your partner's past will help you to cope better with the future.

Identify the positive changes that have taken place in each of your lives and celebrate them together.

8. Family size

At the beginning of the relationship, it is always good to discuss the size of family each of you would prefer. You need to agree about the number of children you hope to have. This will avoid arguments in the future. Don't produce children to impress your parents or to compete with friends, or for any reason other than love. Also find out if there are any problems with childbearing in the wife's family history, or if the wife's family features a lot of twins, or other information, e.g. premature or overdue births may be common in certain families. This will all help you to plan and perhaps know what to expect or to pray against.

9. Health situation

Share together vital information about individual health. Tell each other if there are certain illnesses you or your family suffer from. This will help each of you take these things to God in prayer, and may help you identify diseases sooner so that you can get the right treatment as quickly as possible.

10. Success and failure

Tell each other the successes and failures you have individually experienced in the past or are currently going through. It is possible that where you have failed before your spouse has succeeded in the past and vice-versa. You can learn from individual success and failure to help your home.

11. Advisers

Tell each other who each of you normally consult for advice, whether about spiritual or other issues. This will help the two of you to decide who to go to for advice and counsel in the future.

12. Sex

You need to talk about sex with your partner. You should not deny each other sex. God created it for mutual enjoyment and it is one of the things that makes a marriage unique. Avoid constant complaints of tiredness whenever your spouse asks for sex. You must not use deprivation of sex as a weapon in your marriage, neither should you make unreasonable demands of your partner. Find a happy medium between you of what will please you. For example, if one partner would like it every day but the other once a week, then compromise on three times a week. Be considerate of your spouse's needs. If you don't enjoy sex, you need to pray over it and probably see a counsellor. You should not refuse your spouse sex unless there are genuine health grounds for doing so. Let your spouse know how best you enjoy sex and be ready to do what pleases your spouse, so that you can both derive maximum enjoyment during sex. It is all godly.

BIBLICAL APPROACH TO EFFECTIVE COMMUNICATION IN MARRIAGE

You can have excellent communication in your marriage if you and your spouse can follow the Word of God's wisdom on communication. The following Bible verses will help you and your spouse to become effective communicators at home, and to avoid common difficulties that marriages experience due to communication problems. Meditate on, apply and pray into your life the following Bible verses on a regular basis, and you will see positive changes in the way you and your spouse communicate.

1. The tongue of the learned

> *"The Lord GOD hath given me the tongue of the learned, that I should know how to speak a word in season to him that is weary: he wakeneth morning by morning, he wakeneth mine ear to hear as the learned."* **Isaiah 50:4**

The tongue of the learned is the wisdom of knowing what to say, which comes from studying God's Word. It will help you know how to talk and reply to every comment you receive from your spouse, to bring encouragement, comfort, peace and all good things. With this tongue, your word will always be approved by God.

Prayer point: Father, please give me the tongue of the learned. Help me to know how to talk in every situation, in Jesus' name.

2. Restrained lips

> *"In the multitude of words there wanteth not sin: but he that refraineth his lips is wise."* **Proverbs 10:19**

Restrained lips are those that control what is said. Someone who is in control of their tongue is always brief in their words. Don't open your mouth without thinking about what you are saying first. Many an argument has been caused by hasty words. If you talk too much, you can become irritating to your spouse. And the more you say the greater the risk of being misinterpreted by your spouse. So choose your words carefully and don't wear your partner out by 'talking them to death'! There are also times when you should keep your mouth shut. Some words are not for sharing, as they may do more harm than good.

Prayer point: Father, please give me the grace to control my lips. Perfect my speech in all situations, in Jesus' name.

3. Evil words

> *"Let all bitterness, and wrath, and anger, and clamour, and evil speaking, be put away from you, with all malice..."* **Ephesians 4:31**

A man with an evil heart has an evil tongue. His words betray his character. So the first task is to grow our relationship with God, so that will be no evil in our hearts to overflow out of our lips. But even the holiest of people are tempted to say bad things, so we must keep a tight rein on our lips.

If you can stop yourself from speaking evil words, you will avoid hurting your spouse and prevent arguments with him or her.

Prayer point: Father, please fill my mouth with good words, in Jesus' name. Make me a man/woman of clean lips.

4. Offensive words

> *"For in many things we offend all. If any man offend not in word, the same is a perfect man, and able also to bridle the whole body."* **James 3:2**

Offensive words create fights at home because they annoy and antagonise your spouse. If your words make your spouse angry, you need to change.

Prayer point: Father, please remove offensive words from my mouth and help me to always be pleasant in conversation.

5. Guileless words

> *"For he that will love life, and see good days, let him refrain his tongue from evil, and his lips that they speak no guile: Let him eschew evil, and do good; let him seek peace, and ensue it."* **1 Peter 3:10-11**

A guileless word is a sincere word that has no deception. Avoid speaking a deceptive word to your spouse because you can *"be sure your sin will find you out"* (Numbers 32:23), and one day that word will be exposed. The result will be that you will lose respect and integrity in your spouse's eyes. Your spouse will develop a negative attitude towards you in communication.

Prayer point: Father, please make me a lover of peace and fill my mouth with words that promote life.

6. Wise words

"The mouth of the righteous speaketh wisdom, and his tongue talketh of judgment." **Psalm 37:30**

A wise man speaks wisely and his words gives direction. In this verse, the tongue that talks of "judgement" does not mean criticising others, it means that a wise person says what is just or correct. Your word is supposed to bring solutions to a problem, not make the matter worse.

Prayer point: Father, please make me a speaker of wise words and let my tongue bring solutions in all situations.

7. Promoter of justice

"The law of truth was in his mouth, and iniquity was not found in his lips: he walked with me in peace and equity, and did turn many away from iniquity." **Malachi 2:6**

A promoter of justice is the person who is impartial in conversation, and always speaks what is true. His word also promotes repentance, because when he speaks the receiver sees what is wrong in his own life. Veils are removed through his word. We turn people away from *"iniquity"* not by condemnation but by *"speaking the truth in love"* (Ephesians 4:15).

Prayer point: Father, please make me an agent of justice and put words that give understanding in my mouth

8. Heart of understanding

"Understanding is a wellspring of life unto him that hath it: but the instruction of fools is folly." **Proverbs 16:22**

A heart of understanding will help you to foresee the reaction of your spouse to your style of communication. You will know what to say and what not to say in order to avoid communication breakdown. Your word will not cause emotional disturbance because you avoid certain attitudes during communication. You will know how to talk when your spouse is not in a good mood and what to say when he or she is in high spirits.

Prayer point: Father, please give me a heart of understanding so that I can live peaceably with my spouse.

9. Think before you talk

"The heart of the wise teacheth his mouth, and addeth learning to his lips." **Proverbs 16:23**

Your heart can only teach your mouth how to speak if you think before you speak. Thinking before speaking will enable you to speak from a heart of love and not from negative emotions like anger, jealousy or selfishness. The Holy Spirit whispers the correct, gentle words in our hearts but if we let our emotions rule our lips, we will speak before we have listened to the Spirit. If you can be patient and slow to speak, you will take control of your words.

Avoid speaking hastily because your mouth will be fed by the emotions of your human soul, not your spiritual heart.

Prayer point: Father, please give me a gentle spirit in communication.

10. Pleasant words

> *"Pleasant words are as an honeycomb, sweet to the soul, and health to the bones."* **Proverbs 16:24**

A speaker of pleasant words is an encourager. His word gives strength to the weak. When such a person speaks to a broken heart, the heart is mended. When your spouse is discouraged and afraid, he or she needs words that give hope and increase faith. Be sensitive to your spouse's situation and let your words meet his or her immediate needs.

Prayer point: Father, please make me a speaker of words that give life and promote faith, in Jesus' name.

11. United home

> *"That ye may with one mind and one mouth glorify God, even the Father of our Lord Jesus Christ."* **Romans 15:6**

A home that is united is one where couples reason and think alike. And if they differ on a subject, it is one where they defer to each other and put their partner's feelings first.

But where faith is concerned, they have similar opinions concerning all situations, because they are one with each other and Christ Jesus. The more they become like Him, the more they will be like each other, because they are both learning to imitate Him.

Unity promotes effective communication in marriage. United minds understand each other easily. They speak with one mouth in all important situations. Couples who have been happily married for many years often know what the other one is thinking before they open their mouths, and can finish their spouse's sentence for them (though doing that too often can be irritating!).

Communication breakdown results from a diversity of opinions, with an individual rigidly attached to his or her own opinions, unwilling to shift ground.

Prayer point: Father, please unite me and my spouse both in thought and action. Make us one indeed.

12. Seasoned speech

> *"Let your speech be always with grace, seasoned with salt, that ye may know how ye ought to answer every man."*
> **Colossians 4:6**

Seasoned words edify the hearer. They are attractive. Let your speech be fit for the occasion. Speak words that give direction, not confusion. You will be able to speak with grace if you always consider the other person's feelings before opening your mouth. Then, your answer will be right for the other person, 'leaving a good taste in their mouth' rather than a trail of bitterness or resentment.

Prayer point: Father, please teach me how to use my tongue properly. Make me a speaker of words that build people up rather than tearing them down.

13. Simple declaration

> *"But let your communication be, Yea, yea; Nay, nay: for whatsoever is more than these cometh of evil."*
> **Matthew 5:37**

Let your conversation be simple. Make speech that is easy to understand. Use words that your spouse will easily understand. Also, be a person of integrity in communication so that your spouse trusts your word all the time, which will mean you won't have to swear an oath to establish the truth of a particular statement to your spouse.

14. War of words

> *"The mouth of a righteous man is a well of life: but violence covereth the mouth of the wicked."*
> **Proverbs 10:11**

The word of threat and fear breeds strife. It leads to violence at home. Avoid threatening your spouse during communication. A home where the couple engage in a war of words will not have peace. There will always be uncertainty and heartache.

15. Sound speech

> *"Sound speech, that cannot be condemned; that he that is of the contrary part may be ashamed, having no evil thing to say of you."* **Titus 2:8**

Soundness of speech means honesty and telling the truth, and it is hard to fault. Avoid giving an untruthful reply in response to harsh words from your spouse. If your spouse speaks nastily to you, avoid replying in the same style. Don't repay evil for evil (*Romans 12:17*). Maintain the soundness of your speech in all situations. Soon, you will win your spouse over. Two wrongs can never make a right.

16. Stay with the truth

> *"Hold fast the form of sound words, which thou hast heard of me, in faith and love which is in Christ Jesus."* **2 Timothy 1:13**

In all your conversations with your spouse, maintain speaking the right word and don't drift into the bad language of the world. You must not stop saying words that agree with the gospel. Hold fast to the right word, irrespective of what your spouse is saying to you. By doing so, you will create room for the Holy Spirit to convict your spouse and change his or her behaviour.

Chapter Eight

POWER OF PRAYER

Prayer is a mystery. It is a spiritual exercise. Its operation can't be explained through human understanding. Marriage is also a spiritual entity, because the two people involved in it are spiritual beings. All the problems a marriage will face will have their roots in the things of the spirit.

Marriage is complicated. It can't be handled through human wisdom. You can only solve marital problems permanently through spiritual weapons. If you desire a successful marriage, you need the power of prayer. Through prayer, you will be able to touch those areas of your marriage that the human hand cannot reach.

When you spend time together in prayer as a couple, you will be able to cause the following to happen through the spiritual power of prayer:

1. THERE WILL BE HARMONISATION OF THE SPIRITS

This is a process of bringing your spirit into agreement with your spouse's. This is a silent work of the Holy Spirit. As you pray together, your spirits will become more connected and this will help you to agree naturally on many issues. Couples who pray together find it easy to understand each other. Only the power of prayer can cause such a unity between people of the opposite sex. No human being can make your spirit unite with your spouse's for a successful marital journey.

2. THERE WILL BE MUTUAL UNDERSTANDING

As we have just said, through the power of prayer, you will find it easier to understand each other. The language will be clearer and there will be no twisting of words. Your hearts will be open to each other, especially during communication.

3. YOU WILL BE ABLE TO WIN TOMORROW'S BATTLE TODAY

As you pray together, you will knowingly or unknowingly touch on the issues of the future. This will enable your home to walk in victory. By praying together, you will position your home for victory in every future situation. God's answers to prayer are not limited by time and space.

4. YOU WILL BE ABLE TO PREVENT THE ENEMY FROM PLANTING HIS EVIL SEEDS IN YOUR MARRIAGE

Unity and mutual understanding close the door to the enemy's invasion of your home. Wherever there is unity, the devil flees. As you pray together, you will create the fire of God around your home and this will make the enemy flee from your surroundings.

5. YOU WILL BE ABLE TO CREATE MUTUAL RESPECT IN YOUR RELATIONSHIP

If your spouse is your prayer partner, you will not naturally disrespect him or her. The power of prayer impresses on your mind and that of your spouse that you need each other. This will breed respect naturally.

6. THERE WILL BE CLOSENESS AND OPENNESS

Praying together involves sharing issues together and praying over them. As you bring individual concerns to the prayer altar, you will be creating openness of hearts in your relationship. Indirectly, secrecy will be eliminated in the relationship.

7. YOU WILL BE ABLE TO NATURALLY ELIMINATE INDIVIDUALISM IN YOUR MARRIAGE

Individualism makes a person depend on himself or herself and live a selfish life. Prayer powerfully turns your focus on seeking the good of the other person, rather than just yourself. The comfort of your spouse takes priority in your entire decision-making.

8. YOU WILL CLOSE THE DOOR AGAINST THE ENTRANCE OF A THIRD-PARTY INTO YOUR RELATIONSHIP

Prayer sends out signals to the people in your life that you don't need their help for you and your spouse to live together as a couple. The world will naturally notice that external assistance is not needed in your relationship. This will discourage back-biters, gossips and home destroyers from coming between you and your spouse.

Let us pray

The following prayer points will work wonders in your home if you and your spouse can use them regularly.

1. Pray for the manifestation of the blessings God has reserved for the family in your home, e.g. security, provision, fruitfulness, etc.

2. Pray for God to protect your home against external forces that cause home destruction, e.g. third parties, (people exerting evil influence on your home such as in-laws, neighbours, work colleagues, etc.) demonic spirits, cultural traditions, family traits, that may be at work in the life of either of you.

3. Pray that love will grow between you and your spouse.

4. Pray for that change that you desire in yourself, your spouse, and children or home generally.

5. Pray that God would remove moral weaknesses from the life of your spouse, yourself and your children.

6. Pray that God would teach you how to raise your children in His way.

7. Pray that God would deliver your home from any evil influence that you or your spouse might have passed to your children, and that any generational curses would be broken.
8. Pray that God would help each of your children to marry the right person when they reach marriageable age.
9. Pray that God would make you a submissive wife to your husband or a loving husband to your wife.
10. Pray that God would let your home dwell under the influence of the Spirit of revelation, so that you will be pro-active in nature.
11. Pray against the operation of the spirit that twists word at home and the spirit that sponsors misunderstanding in marriage.
12. Pray that God would fulfil His purposes for your marriage.
13. Pray that God would protect your home against the spirit of separation, either physical or spiritual.
14. Pray that God would break the power of every evil covenant that followed you into marriage.
15. Pray that God would remove from your marriage, any barriers to giving glory to God.
16. Pray that God would help you to fulfil your divine assignment in the life of your spouse – that He would use you to achieve the things He wants for your spouse.
17. Pray that God would protect your children against the spirit of Belial (*1 Samuel 2:12; Judges 10:13*), which seeks

to make children wicked, useless, lawless, good for nothing either to themselves or others.

18. Pray against the invasion of a spirit of contrariness or conflict into your home. You do not want your home invaded by evil forces that cause tension.

19. Pray against evil pressure that would push your home down the wrong path, that God would destroy any such force.

20. Pray that God would protect you from any evil in your home.

21. Pray that God would make your husband a good leader and your wife a good helper.

22. Pray against the spirit that sponsors hatred and suspicion between spouses.

23. Pray that God would protect your home against the influence of other children that would cause rebellion in your children and grief to you and their parents.

24. Pray that God would show mercy on your home, that it would not be judged for the actions of any of your children.

25. Pray that God would protect your home against power struggles between you and your spouse.

26. Pray that God would protect your home against the entrance of the spirit of Jezebel – a domineering spirit.

27. Pray that every evil foundation laid for your home on the day of your marriage would be destroyed by the power of the Holy Spirit.

28. Pray that the heart of your spouse shall not be snatched away from you.

29. Pray that any evil word which has been pronounced against your home is nullified by the power in the blood of Jesus.

30. Pray that God would prevent any evil which has been planned against your home.

31. Pray that any word spoken through any evil tongue to influence you to misbehave, either to your spouse or God, that the blood of Jesus would nullify it.

32. Pray that every satanic agent hired against your home shall fail.

33. Pray that the anointing to prosper in marriage would come upon your home.

34. Pray that God would help you not to be an instrument of destruction in the life of your spouse, but an instrument of His will, and that the devil will not use you to attack your spouse's life.

35. Pray that God would uproot whatever wants to prevent the flow of anointing into your home.

36. Pray that God would strengthen oneness and unity in your home, and that He would give you and your spouse the ability to walk together in all situations (*Amos 3:3*).

37. Pray that God would paralyse any power of household wickedness fashioned against your home.

38. Pray that you and your spouse shall not fall, in Jesus' name.

39. Pray that God would destroy any agent seeking the destruction of your soul and your spouse's soul.

40. Pray that God would plant the seed of divine character in your home.

41. Pray that every humiliation which has been planned by the enemy for your home is broken by the anointing of the Holy Spirit.

42. Pray that God would bring divine solutions to every problem confronting your home.

43. Pray that God would help your family to pray together and stay together.

44. Pray that God would make you a good example to your children.

45. Pray that God would resurrect every good thing which has died in your home by His sovereign power.

46. Pray that all the visions and dreams God has given your home would be fulfilled.

47. Pray that those who are waiting for your home to break shall wait in vain, in Jesus' name.

48. Thank God for your home because the Lord will make it stand.

49. Thank God for your spouse because the Lord will make love grow between you.

50. Thank God for your children because they will all grow to serve the Lord.

51. Thank God for your life because the Lord will make you a good reference point to the world.

BOOKS FROM THE SAME AUTHOR

Journey to the Next Level

The New Creature

Words That Heal

The Winning Dose

This book, and all other books from the same author, are available at Christian bookstores and distributors worldwide.

They can also be obtained through online retail partners such as Amazon or by contacting the author on the address below.

Contacts:
21-23 Stokescroft
Bristol BS1 3PY
United Kingdom

E-mail:
kkasali@yahoo.com

www.ingramcontent.com/pod-product-compliance
Lightning Source LLC
Chambersburg PA
CBHW071926290426
44110CB00013B/1492